# The Photographic Mind

## HOLOGRAPHIC MEMORY SYSTEM

## Dane Spotts

### WITH NANCY ATKINS

A LifeQuest Book/CD Experience  •  Published by LifeQuest Publishing Group  •  Issaquah, Washington

# WARNING

The soundtracks on the CD enclosed with this book use powerful sound technology. If you: have ever suffered from any form of seizure disorder or epilepsy, have ever received any type of head injury or concussion, are currently taking psychoactive drugs such as barbiturates, tranquilizers, or stimulants of any type consult a licensed health professional before using these soundtracks.

Important: The publisher and seller makes no warranty, either expressed or implied, as to the accuracy, effectiveness, or completeness of any of the material contained in this book or of any sound recordings packaged or associated with it; nor does the publisher and seller assume any liability for damages, either incidental or consequential, that may result from the use of the information contained in this book or any of its associated sound recordings.

A LifeQuest Book/CD Experience
Published by LifeQuest Publishing Group
P.O. Box 1444
Issaquah, Washington 98027

LifeQuest Publishing Group
P.O. Box 1444
Issaquah, WA 98027
*lifequest@usa.net*

® *Brain Supercharger* is a registered trademark of Visionary Technology, Ltd.
*Super Memory Transformation, Accelerated Learning Music, Mindscripting Technology, Neuro-Mapping, Neuro-Entrainment Matrix, are all trademarks of Visionary Technology, Ltd.*
All rights reserved.

**Publisher's Cataloging-in-Publication**

Spotts, Dane.
     The photographic mind : holographic memory system / Dane Spotts with Nancy Atkins. -- 1st ed.
     p. cm.
     Includes bibliographical references.
     LCCN: 99-60649
     ISBN: 1-892805-24-3

     1. Memory.  2. Recollection (Psychology)
3. Mnemonics.  I. Atkins, Nancy.  II. Title.

BF385.S66 1999              153.1'2
                           QBI99-1056

Printed in the United States of America
1  2  3  4  5  6  7  8  9  10

# Table of Contents

# Foreword

As more baby-boomers are reaching middle age, record numbers of people are looking for a solution to their aging memory. They are enrolling in memory seminars, eating memory enhancing foods, taking vitamin supplements, undergoing memory evaluations with psychologists, even experimenting with subtle means of expanding memory, such as aromatherapy.

Relax. Your memory is better than you think. And it holds far more potential than you could ever imagine.

The refreshing perspective of the approach taken in *The Photographic Mind* is that any "memory aid" you need for developing this resource you already possess. It is already in your mind and your body—right now. All it takes is the knowledge of how to set it free.

You're about to learn exactly how to do this, with each of your *Photographic Mind Workshops*, which empower you to manage your memory resources using simple effective approaches that deliver immediate results. Day by day you'll see your memory improve. With that improvement your self-confidence will soar.

This will happen for you. When it does, I hope you will pass this book along to a friend who is worrying about their "failing memory." For yours will be a thing of the past.

There is something else too. For as you are about to learn, the inherent value of owning a photographic mind is not in the details you recall, but in the flexible way this information is retained. It's an uncanny ability that lets you intuit the immediate value of information by patterning it against the data organized in your memory banks (more about that idea later).

Developing a photographic mind is a skill. One that will take you way beyond the boundaries that are limiting your potential today. But first, you need to remember where you put your car keys. And that's covered in your first *Photographic Mind Workshop*.

# Introduction & Instructions

## (Please Read First)

*The photographic mind.* It's an alluring concept, isn't it? The ability to have at your command instantly and effortlessly the information that others struggle to remember. Such a skill would seem to be a miraculous and rare gift. But as this book will reveal, having a photographic mind is a gift that can be yours. In fact, it is a gift you already possess.

The challenge however, is for you to develop this gift. And you <u>can</u>—whether you are old or young, a student or highly experienced professional in your field, or perhaps someone who is re-entering the job market after years of raising a family. Thousands of people before you have improved their memory with the powerful systems outlined in this book. You can too. *And, even more amazingly, you will see these dramatic results in a very short period of time.*

There is no such thing as a good memory or a bad memory. There is simply a skilled or an unskilled memory. Memory is not an all-or-none process. It is a matter of degree. People who display exceptional memories should be *admired for their motivation, rather* than *their ability.* The power to remember depends more on <u>learned</u> rather than <u>innate</u> abilities. That's why this program will work for you. Memory is a *trainable skill.* And when trained to a very high degree, your memory can perform amazing feats.

## Why This Book? Why Now?

*The Photographic Mind* applies traditional time-honored memory systems with a new holistic approach based on the latest scientific findings that support the existence of not only an intellectual memory (of your left brain and right brain) but an emotional memory (of your body) as well.

This approach opens up an exciting new dimension to time-proven memory processes to deliver extraordinary powers of recall. Best of all, these are immediate results you'll gain through the *Photographic Mind Workshops* contained in this book. Workshops that engage your total mind and body in incredible feats of memory.

Each workshop is to-the-point, immediately applicable to your everyday environment, and interactive. "Interactive" meaning it allows you to experience (and not just read) the material:

- You'll learn how to animate "mental flip books" in your own memory factory to instantly recall 21 items on a list in their exact order.
- You'll become the architect of your Private Retreat and use the various rooms of your house (and the personal furnishings) as a blueprint for any memory task.
- You'll create your own Virtual Peg Board that gives you the power to recall the rank order of 20 items on a random basis (the 13th, the 6th, the 17th, etc.) as easily as you can access any track on a CD.
- You'll learn how to think in a special language that allows you to code any length number into a word phrase that you just can't forget.
- You'll discover how to picture each of the 52 cards in a deck and use this skill to recall the cards that are already in play, and more importantly, to know which cards are waiting in the deck.

Through the fast-paced and interactive workshops you'll absorb the basics of four separate powerful memory systems effortlessly and quickly. And, best of all, you'll have fun doing it.

## How this Book is Organized

The three parts of the book work together to present the science of memory with the practical application of proven memory systems. It's an entertaining easy-to-learn method that will amaze you with the proof of your memory power.

**Part I gives you a whirlwind tour into the inner workings of the mind**. Drawing on the milestone scientific discoveries of Nobel prize winners over the past two decades as well as from the latest research into Alzheimer's disease, this section delivers you authoritative knowledge on how your memory works and presents this information in clear, concise, everyday language. Filled with exercises and quick side trips into your brain (and into your past), this intriguing, informative journey keeps you involved every step of the way as you delve into your own inner universe.

**After touring your inner universe, Part II takes you to the center of this universe and the heart of this book.** This is the high energy zone that empowers you with knowledge and experience to master the basics of the four memory systems. As you advance from one *Photographic Mind Workshop* to the next, you build your memory powers step-by-step with proven tools and techniques. You can almost feel your brain pulsate as it speeds you light-years ahead into the frontier of your vast memory power.

Here you'll absorb the core memory systems of the course (the Link, the Loci, the Peg, and the Phonetic) through the interactive *Photographic Mind Workshops* that tap into the intellectual memory of your brain and the emotional memory of your body. All the material you need to know is contained in this book.

**Part III accelerates your learning to warp speed with advanced applications of your memory systems.** Drawing on the techniques you learned in Part II, you'll discover a proven method for recalling names with ease. Then you'll revisit your Private Retreat you created in Part II and use your mental blueprint to recite a speech without the use of notecards.

Whether you choose to use the book alone or in tandem with the companion CD, each *Photographic Mind Workshop* offers practical proven methods presented with everyday memory tasks that you can use immediately. You'll see instant results you can use right now in your everyday life. And even better, the unique 3-step learning process makes learning these memory systems fast, easy and fun.

## What's on Your Companion CD?

Enclosed with this book is a very special companion CD with two powerful soundtracks plus an instruction session on how to use them. The first is called *Accelerated Learning Music*™ (located on Track #2). It uses a composition of specially composed largo rhythm music along with affirmations designed to rescript your attitudes and beliefs about memory and learning. As you begin each of the interactive workshops in this book you'll be instructed to play this piece *(Accelerated Learning Music)* in the background while you are doing each lesson.

It is highly recommended that you use these soundtracks while completing each lesson. The *Accelerated Learning Music* soundtrack uses a special mix of brain boosting music with mindscripting™ affirmations designed to enhance learning. This soundtrack is based on accelerated learning research done by Bulgarian scientist Georgi Lasonaov along with the Mozart studies conducted in 1993 at the University of California. It was discovered that specific rhythm, harmonic, and melodic characteristics of certain musical forms enhances your receptivity for learning. Medical science backs up this idea with studies suggesting that music with a pulse of 40 to 60 beats per minute can shift your consciousness from the normal waking state of "beta brain waves" to the slower "alpha range brain waves" (associated with relaxation), which in turn slows down the body and mind and this too appears to strengthen memory.

Listening to this music is similar to exercising for higher brain functioning. It causes your mind and body to resonate to its relaxing tones and textures as it improves your ability to concentrate. It does this by lending a structure of organization to the incoming information. The *Accelerated Learning Music* soundtrack playing in the background during the workshops is designed to help you concentrate and focus as the music slows and equalizes your brainwaves to increase your mental organization. Scientists call this "whole brain synchrony" and believe it to be the optimum state for learning and retaining new information.

The second soundtrack on your CD (located on Track #3) is titled *Super Memory Transformation*™ and it uses the *Brain Supercharger*® technology to drive your brain into a peak state of receptivity for learning, while rescripting your attitudes and beliefs about learning and memory. You'll use this soundtrack as you complete each lesson to deeply relax both your mind and body and help lock the new lesson material into memory.

The *Brain Supercharger* technology is also designed to expand your level of awareness and through regular use will allow you to access higher states of consciousness. Training your brain to enter into these dream-like states can have enormous benefits. Users have reported reduced stress, enhanced creativity, peak experiences, and feelings of psychological well-being. Psychologists believe the mind uses these altered states for psychological programming as well as healing both mind and body.

As I report in my book, *Super Brain Power: 28 Minutes to a Supercharged Brain*, researchers believe this special altered state opens a window into the unconscious where it's possible to implant positive programming. And because you're in a more relaxed and suggestible mind state, this new programming has a better chance to stick.

Over 500,000 recordings incorporating the *Brain Supercharger* technology have been distributed around the world, and there are a number of titles available for programming various aspects of your life.

**(For more information on how to use your CD and the *Brain Supercharger* technology see the Appendix on page 233.)**

## The Easy 3-Step Active-Passive Learning Process

*The Photographic Mind* is a comprehensive program that builds your confidence and memory power as you progress from one workshop to the next. Each *Photographic Mind Workshop* is presented with a unique 3-step format to help:

- accelerate your learning &
- relax your mind and body to better assimilate each lesson.

Of course, a main benefit of the *Photographic Mind Workshops* is that you can adjust the pace of the program to fit your individual needs. To achieve the best results, you should proceed through all three steps of each workshop in one sitting (approximate time: 60 minutes per lesson). Here's a quick breakdown of each step:

• **Step One—Active Learning Session**

As you read through each lesson you'll be participating in an interactive learning process which allows you to learn through the direct experience of your senses. You'll read along in your book and recite—*out loud*—the material you are learning. By engaging your different senses you dramatically increase your capacity for boosting your memory.

During the Active Learning Session you should be playing the *Accelerated Learning Music* (Track #2 on your CD) while reading the material. At the beginning of each workshop the following reminder will be displayed to let you know it's time to turn on your CD player.

**To enhance your experience of the material please play the *Accelerated Learning Music* soundtrack (located on Track #2 of your *Brain Supercharger* CD) while you complete the following workshop exercise.**

• **Step Two—Passive Learning Session (Plugging in to the *Brain Supercharger* Technology)**

Here's where the *The Photographic Mind* system differs substantially from all other memory books and courses. What you're about to experience is a true breakthrough in mind development technology. After you've completed your active work with each lesson you'll do what is called a "Passive Learning Session." You'll put down your book and don a pair of stereo headphones. Cue up Track #3 which is the *Super Memory Transformation* soundtrack that uses the *Brain Supercharger* technology and push play. Close your eyes, lay back and allow the special frequency matrix of the *Brain Supercharger* to massage your brain and put you into a deep meditative state of relaxed awareness.

What does it feel like? Some have described it as feeling like you've left your body and entered into another dimension. Whatever your experiences might be the time you spend with your *Brain Supercharger* CD will not only be a welcome "time out" from your lesson, but will have many side benefits.

At the beginning of each Passive Learning Session you'll see the following paragraph as highlighted below...

**To help lock-in your lesson please play the *Super Memory Transformation* Soundtrack (located on Track #3 of your *Brain Supercharger* CD). Put the book aside for now and make sure to use stereo headphones. Find a comfortable position & quiet place where you can rest undisturbed for the next 30 minutes.**

This tells you it's time to plug into your *Brain Supercharger* for your 30 minute "relax & learn" session. Again the point of doing this is the powerful audio technology incorporated into this soundtrack not only relaxes both your mind and body but assists you in assimilating the information from the lesson you've just covered. Scientific research suggests that learning is enhanced when your mind is relaxed. In addition this soundtrack incorporates state-of-the-art mindscripting technology for assisting you in reprogramming your memory powers and helping accelerate the learning process by locking the material into permanent memory.

Plus, as an added benefit to this process, you'll find that you'll come out of this second step feeling totally relaxed, refreshed and ready to take on the day.

> ## NOTE:
>
> The *Brain Supercharger* technology incorporated into your *Super Memory Transformation* soundtrack uses special sound frequencies to redirect the energies of consciousness. It is a potent tool for transformation and learning. However for some users these effects may be too powerful to allow them to proceed into Step 3 immediately after doing a session. As this is experimental mind technology it is recommend that you test it out first and see how well you respond. If you discover that after doing a session you are unable to continue on to Step 3 and complete the assessment exercise(s) you can choose to skip your *Brain Supercharger* session until AFTER you've completed Step 3.

### • Step Three—Assessment

This is where you measure your progress. At the end of each workshop you'll take a brief quiz and see how well you perform before moving on to the next lesson.

## The Power of You, the Power of Now

The memory systems in this course have literally changed the lives of people who have integrated them into their daily thinking. This can happen for you—beginning today, beginning right now.

Remember, each of your *Photographic Mind Workshops* builds on the skill level you gained in the previous workshop. Therefore, please proceed through the workshops in the order they are presented AND complete all the exercises associated with each individual memory system before continuing to the next system.

Congratulations on taking the action to improving your memory. It's a simple act that will benefit you everyday for the rest of your life. And it all begins in Part I in a celebration of discovery that shows you why:

- You already possess the gift of a multi-dimensional architecture of holographic memory.
- You already have the groundwork of a total command system of access routes connecting you to the information you need to know—quickly and easily.

What you need is the knowledge of how to tap into the left and right brain of your intellectual memory, along with the emotional memory of your body to open the floodgates of your memory power. The four powerful memory systems included in this book will give you this knowledge through a fun and entertaining interactive experience.

Are you ready to access the virtually unlimited memory gifts of your photographic mind? Then let's begin.

# PART I
# How Your Memory Works

# The Untapped Potential of Your Mind

Most of us are acquainted with someone who has an exceptional memory, or have seen incredible feats of memory performed on television talk shows, in business seminars, or even at the card table. Yet even "everyday memory" is a wonderful ability.

Think of the many ways you depend on your memory every hour of the day—to recall people's names and their phone numbers, to remember meeting times, to remind yourself of birthdays and anniversaries, to cover the major points in speeches and sales presentations—not to mention the more trivial but none-the-less necessary ongoing memory tasks such as knowing the items on a shopping list, where you last put your keys, and remembering to mail your bills and take your clothes to the dry cleaners.

Yes, we all get frustrated with our memory from time to time, but just imagine how impossible life would be if you didn't have the ability to remember at all. It would be as if you were doing everything for the first time—from driving the car to using a copy machine to tying your shoes in the morning. Without the resource of your memory, you would need to respond to every situation as if you had never experienced it before. And even worse, you wouldn't have a sense of who you are because you wouldn't have any recollections from childhood, nor the ability to reason and make judgments based on previous experience.

Your memory is a wonderful gift. *Don't curse it—celebrate it.* And imagine how incredible this gift of memory will be when you increase your powers by 200%, then 300%, then 400% and even up to 500%. But it is important for you to know right now that you have an incredible resource of memory available to you—even in its "untrained" condition.

## Can You Remember This?

Take a moment right now to marvel at the memory powers you currently have in your ability to recall the following:

- scenes from early birthday parties or family holidays
- street names from your old neighborhood
- your past teachers' names
- your first kiss
- your first phone number
- how to ride a bike
- how to recite the Pledge of Allegiance

Even if you haven't had the need to call up this information in years, you will find that some or most of these memories are there for you. And what's even more amazing is that you are able to pull all of this information out of an *untrained* memory—"untrained" meaning that no one ever sat down with you and explained *how* to remember.

In this course you will learn step-by-step how to boost your memory far beyond your present capability with three powerful memory systems. Each system will increase your ability to perform the three functions of memory—record, retain and retrieve—and in so doing allow you to tap into the immense reservoir of power that is at your mental fingertips.

Your two pound brain can store more than today's most advanced computers—*we're talking about billions and billions of bits of information*. And the exciting part is that most of us are using only the surface level of our memory abilities. There is so much more power there for you. The simple and effective memory systems in this course will let you tap into that power *naturally* with processes and techniques that work in the same manner as your brain to quickly and easily expand your memory power.

Each of the systems presented in this course (Link, Loci, Peg and Phonetic) is effective in and of itself. But when applied together these systems essentially create a multi-dimensional architecture of memory that is constantly seeking or searching your environment to record, retain, and retrieve data and stimuli for you.

It's as if these systems implant thousands of cameras in your body—constantly in motion—zooming in and zooming out—clicking hundreds of pictures every second to record stimuli from your environment. These pictures are then sent to any number of your internal networks that scan and share the pictures with other networks to satisfy the natural need of the brain to make sense of the information it is receiving.

A basic tenant of this course is that your mind is constantly seeking to know "the why" behind any data or stimuli received from your environment—*seeking to know "why" by developing patterns or categories and cross-referencing one category to another*. The purpose of these categories is not just to make sense of the information, the purpose of these categories is also to aid in the recall of the information—*to give you a total command system of access routes that will connect you with the information you want to retrieve—quickly and easily.*

This is not science fiction. This is your gift of memory. The final frontier is not "outer space" but your own "inner space," which is a miraculous place you can come to know in the workshops through out this book. It is truly exciting territory for all who are open to coming into this legacy of gifted memory. And that last phrase cannot be emphasized enough: *for all who are open to coming into this legacy of gifted memory.* Are you seeing that you have a beautiful memory? Are you feeling that the power is in you to expand your memory capabilities exponentially? You need to believe it before it can happen for you. But if you're not quite comfortable with the idea yet, relax. You're not alone.

## Overcoming 3 Psychological Blocks to Memory

Many people who want to increase their memory power simply cannot do so until they rid themselves of three psychological blocks which put an artificial ceiling on their advancement.

• **The first psychological block is the critical-logical block**. It tries to tell you that it just isn't possible for you to expand your memory by 500% or more because it sounds too fantastic. Another slant to this block is that, while you believe these powerful memory systems can work for *others*, you doubt that they can work for *you*.

• **The second psychological block is the intuitive/emotional block**. This block is the result of years and years of conditioning from previously bad experiences that have emotionally triggered you into accepting a low evaluation of your ability to memorize. This block may be the result of poor grades on tests that relied solely on your memorization of facts by REPEATING and REPEATING the information over and over again. This act of REPETITION is the poorest method of memorization and is no indication of the true ability you do have. Let go of those feelings. They aren't valid. The ability to recall facts, names and places, even hour-long speeches is within you when you harness the natural processes of the powerful systems in this course.

• **The third block to overcome in boosting your memory power is the ethical/moral block**. It tries to convince you that the techniques of this course must not be valid because they appear to be too easy. But look at the opposite. Trying to memorize is hard work—and it doesn't work. *So try something new.* Try the opposite—try to relax and have fun to aid your memory. That is exactly what the systems in this course ask of you—to relax, to let go of the stress and the boredom of memorization.

Many people are surprised at the incredible powers of memory that this program allows them to command. But, rather than be surprised, you should feel expectant of these incredible results. By being expectant, you position your mind for success from the start. Two techniques to help you achieve this mind frame are visualization and the use of affirmations.

## Visualization Session: How to Relax Your Mind and Body

Visualization is the process of using your imagination to create a mental picture in your mind's eye of that which you want to experience. It's the process of playing a movie in your head that allows you to see, feel, hear, taste and touch the outcome you desire.

Used by Olympic champions, stock market experts, actors and more, visualization lets you tap into your natural ability to imagine in a more conscious way. Athletes use visualization in advance of the sporting event to rehearse and perfect their moves in their mind. Stock market experts and other professionals use visualization to vividly imagine a successful outcome to a business decision. Likewise, great actors and entertainers of all types use this tool to envision their great performance and hear the clapping of the audience in request of an encore. In all these examples, visualization is tapping into the power of the imagination to bring forth a desired goal into reality.

The goal you desire as you begin this program is to simply keep your mind open and to be expectant of the incredible results you can achieve through these workshops. A main element in creating this mind frame is to relax your body and mind. Through a visualization exercise you can learn to do this easily and quickly.

Visualization is a simple tool. Yet, because of this simplicity, there is a tendency for our rational, intellectual mind to analyze and dismiss its powerful effects. It is important for you to devote yourself exclusively to the short time it takes to complete a visualization exercise. By paying attention to the exercise, instead of planning your dinner or what you'll wear to an upcoming event, you can achieve the desired outcome of an open and expectant mind.

 • **The first step in visualization is to get into a comfortable position, close your eyes, and focus on your breathing.** With your eyes closed, roll them upwards slightly, as if you're trying to see the center of your forehead, and listen to yourself breathe. Focus your attention on slowly taking deep breaths, and on the sound of the air coming in and out of your lungs. Feel yourself relax. Do this breathing five times. It will only take 45 seconds. This is a simple relaxation exercise that mentally calms your mind as it relaxes your body to prepare you for the second step in this exercise.

• **The second step is to select an image that creates a soothing feeling in your mind.** Calm and peaceful scenes from nature are especially helpful in erasing worries and distractions.

Most people find that listening to the sound of waves or walking along a white sandy beach is a wonderful way to relax. The following words describe such a scene. As you read the words, use all your senses to bring the scene alive in your mind and body. Your senses are the tools of your imagination. The more you can see, feel, hear, smell, and even taste the sensations in the following scene, the easier it will be for you to visualize yourself on this beach, and in so doing, create the relaxed mind frame you desire.

> *You are walking on a beautiful beach.*
> *Feel the warmth of the sun.*
> *Feel the warmth of the sand under your feet and notice how*
>     *it gently trickles between your toes as you walk.*
> *Savor the blue sky and the blueness of the water.*
> *Now begin to walk towards that water.*
> *As you walk along the edge of the water feel the waves*
>     *gently lapping around your ankles.*
> *Feel a light breeze upon your face and feel your cares and*
>     *worries gently drifting away.*
> *In the distance, you can hear sea gulls calling to each*
>     *other.*
> *You see a lone sailboat on the horizon.*
> *And closer to shore, you see the sparkling pattern of the sun*
>     *on the water.*

Enjoy this scene for a few minutes. Feel an inner calm soothe your mind, releasing you from distracting worries, cares, and pressures. Come away from this experience gently. Count down from 5 to 1. Slowly become aware of your present surroundings. Feel your body switch on as you look around your environment. Stretch and take a few deep breaths. You now feel rested. You now feel relaxed. You are ready to begin the Affirmation Session.

## Affirmation Session: How to Reprogram Your Mind

An affirmation states that something you desire is already a reality. It is similar to the technique of goal setting, except that it states the goal as having already been achieved. This simple but powerful difference allows you to reach your goals much quicker, because your mind already believes it has achieved success. It just goes about creating the external circumstances to match the internal reality. Although it seems too simple to work, it is very powerful stuff.

The way to use affirmations is easy. First, you identify a specific problem you're having. Then you write a short sentence that states the desired outcome of the problem as having already been achieved. The last step is to say the affirmation out loud to yourself, and to repeat it several times a day.

To understand how this simple process can be so powerful requires you to have a basic understanding of how your mind operates. You have a conscious (the objective, rational mind) and a unconscious (the subjective, irrational mind). The two most important things to remember about this duality of mind are:

- The conscious mind rules your waking reality and it based on logic and rational thinking.
- The unconscious (or subconscious) is the source your attitudes and behavior. And it cannot tell the difference between a real and an imagined experience.

*The unconscious mind directs your behavior based on what it believes and accepts to be true. It sees each thought and image as an instruction of how to proceed and on a totally unconscious basis goes about creating an external reality to match these inner images and beliefs. Therefore, when you control your thoughts (how you see yourself and the world), you begin a process that shapes your "inner" images of reality and this affects your external experience.*

Affirmations are designed to help you "reprogram" your unconscious into thinking that the positive outcome you want has already occurred. This process works because, as you already learned, your unconscious cannot tell the difference between something that is imagined and something that already exists.

The affirmations in this upcoming exercise are designed to help reprogram your thinking in two ways. The first way is to de-suggest yourself of any bad feelings you may harbor over your memory. The second is to open your mind to receiving the dramatic gains of this program. Again this may seem over simplistic but by saying these affirmations out loud (at least once a day) you are helping to overcome the psychological blocks that may be limiting your memory powers.

I learn quickly
I have instant recall of everything I read
All knowledge is available to me
I am wisdom
I am an advanced learner
I am learning faster each day
I like to learn new things
My IQ goes up
I am intelligent and wise
I learn faster each day
I like to read
I am articulate and knowledgeable
I read faster and remember more
I am a student of life
Learning new things comes easily for me
I discover
I am a quick study
I am relaxed and calm
I am wisdom and learning
I remember everything
When I learn new information I focus my attention
I learn faster than others because I'm focused
My memory improves daily
People around me are amazed at my ability to learn
    so quickly
I accelerate my learning
I can do it
I read faster and remember more
I remember everything I see
New concepts come easily for me
I see how things connect
I have an excellent memory
My reading comprehension goes up
I have instant recall
My memory improves
The more I read the quicker I learn
I am an unlimited person
My mind serves me well

Now come away from this experience gently. Count down from 5 to 1. Slowly become aware of your present surroundings. Feel your body switch on as you look around your environment. Stretch and take a few deep breaths.

*Note: All the affirmations which are listed on the previous page are also used on your Brain Supercharger CD to help you program a new attitude and belief system about your memory.*

• **Feedback on your visualization and affirmation session:**

> Do you feel rested?
> Do you feel expectant of your memory abilities?
> Or are you at this point a bit skeptical about the potential of
>    your memory power?

If the last statement applies to the way you're feeling right now, just relax. The affirmations you heard may seem quite fantastic to you now. But once you get just the first inkling of your potential memory power, you will be able to let go of any doubts you now hold. By the end of this course you will embrace these seemingly miraculous affirmations with a show of uncanny memory powers whose demonstrable results will fulfill every promise these affirmations hold for you—regardless of how undeveloped your power of recall appears to be at this point.

# Basic Mnemonics

The four memory systems presented in this course are tried and proven time-honored memory processes. The oldest system dates back to 500 B.C. to the time of the Greek and Roman orators who relied on its powers to deliver speeches with unfailing accuracy—without the use of modern day conveniences we use such as notecards or cue cards.

Collectively these systems belong to a body of knowledge called *mnemonics*. This word is derived from Mnemsoyne, the name of the ancient Greek goddess of memory. Today, mnemonics refers in general to methods for improving memory.

## Rhymes and Associations

We've all been exposed to mnemonics at one time or another. These can be unusual specific memory aids or techniques, such as the spelling rule "i" before "e" except after "c." Or rhymes such as "In fourteen hundred and ninety-two Columbus sailed the ocean blue."

In addition to using rhymes, we also try to aid our memory by connecting the new information to something we already know. This method is known as "association." It links together in a logical fashion something you know with something you don't know. An example of this memory trick is the use of each letter in the word HOMES to recall the five Great Lakes—H for Huron, O for Ontario, M for Michigan, E for Erie and S for Superior.

## Music, Rhythm and Chunking

Mnemonics often use music and rhythm to help remember a string of non-related items, such as the alphabet. To this day, you probably still sing the ABCs to help you locate the beginning letter of a word you are looking up in a dictionary.

The ABC song also uses another method called "chunking," which breaks up the string of single items into clumps of information for easier recall. As you mentally sing the ABC song you will notice this chunking effect: A, B, C, D, E, F, G......H, I, J, K, ...L, M, N, O, P......Q, R, S...T, U, V...W, X... Y and Z. Scientists say we can hold seven bits of information in our short-term memory. A common example of this logic is the seven digit telephone number. Yet, it also uses the chunking method to break the number into two chunks—a three part chunk followed by a four part chunk.

An enhanced method of the chunking technique is to take nonsense numbers or letters and make them meaningful. For example, to help you remember a 1-800 phone number, many companies turn some or all of the numbers into letters that have a tie in to their company. It is much easier to remember 1-800-STARBUC for Starbucks Coffee than the number 1-800-782-7282.

This is also the same principle behind the many acronyms such as IBM and AT&T. Interestingly enough, some acronyms become so commonplace that they actually become part of our language as a bona-fide word—for example, "scuba" is really an acronym for "self-contained underwater breathing apparatus." Acronyms are very effective ways of chunking information to make it easier to remember.

## Going Beyond Mnemonics

The mnemonic devices of rhyme, music, association and chunking are helpful because they either work with the way your mind thinks, or build on what you already know. *Yet they are limiting because they can't expand to include the horrendous amount of information you need to know.*

Can you imagine trying to come up with a rhyme or clever word association for everything you need to remember? It just isn't practical or even feasible. These rhymes and word associations are too logical, and not flexible enough to easily bring together what you <u>need</u> to know, with what you <u>already</u> know in a quick and easy manner.

These techniques are not bad, they are just limited. And because they are limited they are limiting you—in your ability to remember names, in your ability to recall lists of items, in your ability to recite speeches with unfailing accuracy, and in your ability to record, retain and retrieve the massive amount of data and stimuli you are bombarded with from your environment every minute of the day.

The true power and capacity of your memory lies underneath the surface of your memory as you now know it. The four powerful memory systems of this course are mnemonic *processes*, which unlike these examples of specific mnemonic *aids*, are incredibly expandable and flexible for use in remembering names, procedures, speeches, playing cards—virtually any body of information you need to know.

These systems are time-honored processes. Many people before you have used them to discover the virtually limitless memory capacity of their mind. These systems are also the foundation of every effective book or course on memory improvement today. But unlike other books or courses, this program is designed to give you an "open sesame" approach in the application of these systems. This is a *natural holistic approach* that allows you to release your potential memory powers through more efficient and less stressful ways than with a traditional memory course.

# The Intellectual Memory of Your Left & Right Brain

In 1983, Roger Sperry of the California Institute of Technology won the Nobel Prize for his discovery that the two distinctive hemispheres of the brain (the left and the right) had specialized functions. The holistic approach to memory used in this course invites the participation of your left brain (the logical/verbal mind) and your right brain (the visual/musical mind) and your body. The secret to its success is to keep the left brain, right brain and body working together to harmonize and support each other in the memory process.

For example, mnemonics can be either visual or verbal. Traditional mnemonics involve the verbal process of the left brain in which you learn or memorize through words. An earlier example was with the association of the word HOMES to remember the names of the five Great Lakes.

When you are learning or memorizing through pictures, you are engaging the visual process of the right brain. Visual mnemonics use pictures as clues instead of words. Visual mnemonics is the principle behind the concept of the title of this course—*The Photographic Mind*. The basic premise here is that we think in pictures and not words.

Let me give you an example. When you hear the word HOUSE, for instance, what do you think of? Do you see the word house? Or do you see a *visual image* of a house? Now imagine hearing the word DOG. Do you see the letters D-O-G, or a visual image of a dog? Most people see a picture, not the word.

Indeed, using pictures as a cue was how we learned to speak. Our parents pointed to objects and said the name—cup, juice, clock, car, moon. It wasn't until years later that we began to read the words of the objects that we first "read" as pictures. It's not that you cannot see the words DOG or HOUSE in your mind— it's just that your first thought when you hear the word is a visual image.

---

### Do You Get the Picture?

Scientific research has shown that our capacity for pictures may be almost unlimited. In one study, people were shown 2,560 different pictures over a period of several days. Later, these same people were shown 280 *pairs* of *pictures*, with one of the pictures in each pair having been one they were shown previously. They were then asked to identify the picture in each pair that they had been shown before. Amazingly, the people were able to identify the correct picture 90% of the time. *And three months later when the same people were asked again to identify the correct picture, the accuracy rate was still very high.*

---

Our ability to remember pictures is uncanny. And so is our ability to conjure up an image in our mind. How do we do it? With our imagination. When you hear the word DOG, you can see a dog in your mind's eye because of your ability to imagine one. The stronger your imagination, the more vivid the picture appears.

## If You Can Imagine it, You Can Remember it

Imagination is a playful, free-flowing resource that takes the hard work out of memory tasks. It replaces the stress (from rote memorization) with fun as you visualize the information you want to remember.

It makes memory an exciting process. This is the process of developing a photographic mind by involving your left brain, your right brain and your whole body to record, retain and retrieve the knowledge and stimuli from your environment in such a way that you can freely access it in an instant.

For example, take the word APPLE. You are going to the store and you want to buy apples. The right side of the brain sees the image of the apple and the left side of the brain can see the written word APPLE. When you get to the store you can recall APPLE by seeing either the image or the word in your mind. The benefit here is that any information that is processed in two ways—by both the left and right brain—is more likely to be remembered than if it is represented in only one way. With *dual representation*, as this is called, you are twice as likely to be able to retrieve the message.

APPLE is an example of a concrete word—it's an object that is easily visualized. Test after test has shown that concrete words are remembered much better than abstract verbal words—such as nourishment, management, motivation. The reason concrete words are more easily remembered is because you can vividly picture them in your mind. The reason why the brain cannot easily recall abstract words is because these words (such as NOURISHMENT) are simply not as easy to picture.

The importance of this concept is that if you can't picture these words, then you aren't leaving a memory trace in your right brain where the visual imagery process takes place. Therefore, you are only leaving a memory in your left "verbal" brain. With only one trace, or message, you aren't as likely to recall the information.

The main benefit here to improving your memory is that information which can be visualized has twice the likelihood of being recalled because it can be processed by both sides of your brain—the left side processing the verbal words and the right side processing the visual images. It is as though you are cross-referencing the information to be retrieved under two categories—a verbal category and a visual category, giving you dual representation.

## Succeeding in the Three Stages of Memory

Studies by research scientists have revealed that the memory process can be broken down into three distinct stages of recording, retaining and retrieving. In understanding how memory works through these stages it is helpful to draw an analogy between filing a memory in your brain and filing a memo in a filing cabinet.

For example, in the first stage you record information (a memo) on a piece of paper. Next comes retain. You put this memo in the file drawer under the appropriate heading of MEMO. Then comes retrieval. When you want the memo you simply go to your file cabinet and pull out the MEMO file.

Now, imagine this is a very important memo to your boss justifying your need for a raise based on your accomplishments. You want to be sure you don't lose this memo. So you make an extra copy of it and file it under PERSONAL. In essence, you have cross-referenced the memo in two places to be sure you can find it.

Similarly, you can cross-reference material you want to remember by putting that information in the visual right brain and the verbal left brain. This, again, is dual representation where the information is networked between the two halves of your brain which are working together in harmony. And too, it is one component of the holistic approach to memory as used in the workshops in this book—using the left and right brain to support each other in the function of memory.

Here you begin to see the architecture of your memory rising up from its foundation. The left brain and the right brain are reaching out like two halves of a bridge to span a river. There are pilings being driven down into the water for support. There are huge steel girders being raised into place. There are guide wires connecting each section for strength as each side extends out to connect with the other and open up an information highway into the universe in your mind.

## Why We Forget

To remember anything you need to succeed at all three stages of recording, retaining and retrieving. Yet to forget something you only need to fail at one of these stages. Each stage has its own roadblocks. The first step to overcoming these roadblocks is to learn about them.

• **Stage One.** In the recording stage, the most common roadblock to remembering is a lack of attention. Most of the time you simply aren't focused on what is being said, or on what you are doing. In these cases, it is not a matter of forgetting, because you simply didn't record the information in the first place.

A classic example is forgetting where you laid your car keys when you came in the house because you were focused on another activity—such as checking your phone or e-mail messages, or opening the mail. This is a breakdown actually before you get into the recording stage. In a word, you are being *absent-*

*minded*—you are "absent of mind." or your mind was focused on something other than what you were doing.

You can really only consciously pay attention to one thing at a time. When you are so-called "doing two things at once," you are really switching your attention back and forth rather than simultaneously doing the two together.

What else can go wrong in the recording stage? Something called *distortion*, meaning you remember things the way you want to remember them. This suggests that what you record is affected by your own values and interests.

---

### Recalling A Fake Memory

This exercise is a good example of the power of distortion in memory. The following list does not contain the word TURKEY, but most people who are asked to repeat the list (after hearing the words read aloud) add the word TURKEY.

Try this one on your friends. Recite the following words out loud to a friend and ask them to repeat as many as they can remember: *Thanksgiving, stuffing, eat, dinner, family, yams, pie, giblets, gravy, cook, taste, simmer.* People often add the word TURKEY—not because they heard it, but due to the fact they "felt" it should be included because it is so closely related.

---

• **Stage Two**. One explanation for why we forget in the second stage of memory is due to *decay*. This theory suggests that memories cause a physical trace in the brain that gradually decays or fades away with time. The reason it fades is because it wasn't a vivid memory in the first place, or it hasn't been called up enough times. And just as with a trail in the woods, the less it's used the more difficult it becomes to find.

Another theory for what can go wrong in the retaining stage is *repression*. This theory of Sigmond Freud suggests that unpleasant or unacceptable memories may be forgotten intentionally. They are pushed into the unconscious on purpose so that the person will not have to live with them. While this may explain the most emotional of experiences, it doesn't give us much insight into the day-to-day forgetfulness we experience.

• **Stage Three**. Most memory breakdowns occur in the third stage of retrieval. We just can't "find" the information. Just as sometimes you can't find the file in your file cabinet, you sometimes can't locate the access to a specific memory.

However, retrieval is a function of how well the data was recorded and retained in the first place. Therefore, when you improve the degree to which you record and retain information, you automatically boost your ability to retrieve information. The three systems in this course will show you how to record and retain information and stimuli from your environment with a total command system of access routes to connect you with the information you want to retrieve, and you'll be able to do so quickly and effortlessly. And because these memory systems work with your long-term memory (as opposed to your short-term memory) the memory becomes permanent.

## The Difference Between Long-Term and Short-Term Memory

Short-term memory is defined by psychologists as "working memory," which is capable of recording seven elements for a maximum of 30 seconds. It refers to your attention span, or how much you can consciously pay attention to at one time. In continuing the file cabinet analogy, short-term memory can be compared to your in-basket, while long-term memory is your file cabinet.

Short-term memory is easily disrupted. You use short-term memory when you look up a phone number and then dial it immediately. For instance, if you look up a phone number, and then someone asks you a question as you start to dial it— what happens? You most likely will forget the number. This can be very frustrating. But actually, this rapid forgetting rate of short-term memory serves a purpose. Here's why:

• **It alleviates traffic jams in your thinking by dispatching data as soon as you use it.** In this way short-term memory serves as a temporary scratch pad allowing you to retain immediate results as you think and solve problems. Imagine how cluttered and jumbled your mind would be if you were consciously aware of every little bit of information your mind recorded.

• **It helps you maintain your current picture of the world around you.** Short-term memory indicates to you what objects are out there and where they are located. By maintaining and constructing these "world frames," your short-term memory keeps your visual perceptions realistic—updating them as you go.

Now let's look at long-term memory—your big cabinet full of file drawers. This refers to information you retain for a few minutes, a few days, or many years. Psychologists believe long-term memory is composed of several different types.

> • The first type is <u>procedural</u> long-term memory, such as involved in remembering how to do a skill, such as driving a car or tying your shoe.
>
> • A second type is <u>episodic memory</u>, referring to personal events, such as where you were when you heard Princess Diana had been killed, or recalling a happy time such as a childhood birthday party.
>
> • A third type of long-term memory is <u>semantic memory</u>. This includes the factual information such as math equations or word meanings that really don't have a connection to time or place. In other words, this means that you don't remember when or where you learned the information.

Of the three types of long-term memory, psychologists have found that one consistently has the poorest rate of recall. Based on your own long-term memory experience, which type of recall gives you the most difficulty—remembering how to perform a skill, recollecting personal events, or reciting factual knowledge?

If you're like most people, the last one, or semantic memory, gives you the most difficulty. The reason why is because there are no emotions associated with it. And the key to remembering facts is to imbue them with emotions.

Unlike short-term memory, long-term memory is virtually unlimited. As mentioned earlier, it is more powerful than the most advanced computers in the world, capable of storing billions and billions of pieces of information. Also, unlike short-term memory, long-term memory is not easily disrupted.

The drawback to long-term memory is retrieval. Again, using the analogy of the in-basket to short-term memory, when you want to access information in short-term memory you just dump everything out and you will find it quickly because short-term memory holds such a limited amount of data. This is not the case with long-term memory. You just can't dump it. What you need is a systematic search tool to find the file you need.

But again, retrieval is a function of how the data was retained in the first place. *Imagine if you were to simply throw your files into the cabinet and close the drawer.* They would be in your file cabinet, yes, but when stored in a haphazard manner would you be able to access a specific file quickly? Not likely.

The same is true for the way many people store information in their minds. They just absorb the information like a sponge and hope they can wring it out of their brain when the time comes to use it again. But there are better ways, as you will learn in the memory systems taught in the *Photographic Mind Workshops.* Best of all, none of the systems here use rote memorization. And there are several reasons why this is so.

## The Double Curse of Rote Memorization

Rote memorization is simply the act of repeating and repeating information over and over again until you are able to remember it. It has a double disadvantage in that it is both ineffective and boring. The reason for both of these is because this process doesn't include you in the picture.

> *It doesn't engage your mind.*
> *It doesn't invite you to come to know that which you are to*
>    *memorize.*
> *It leaves YOU out.*

Pure memorization requires an empty vacuum state in which nothing exists except the material which is to be memorized. This information is floating around detached from the environment. Your role is to be a consumer of knowledge whereby you focus on it long enough to burn it into your brain through

REPEAT—REPEAT—REPEAT.

And what happens? You forget. Why? Because it wasn't memorable. "What?" you're thinking. "Of course it wasn't memorable because if it was I would have remembered it." Precisely. So the challenge here is not to memorize in an empty vacuum state, but to play with that information in a way that lets you reconnect with it—*making it memorable*. Through this process you become a creator of knowledge, rather than a consumer. This puts you right in the middle of the action and involves you in the process.

The way to do that is to mentally visualize the information with your right brain in pictures. And then put yourself into the picture. *In other words, to use both sides of your brain to achieve dual representation of the information through the visual imagery process of the right brain and the verbal process of the left brain*. This is known as the *intellectual memory* of the mind.

But there's more. There is also an emotional memory of the body. It is the other element in this holistic approach to memory of left brain, right brain and body. And its ability to lock in memories is the greatest power of all.

# The Emotional Memory of Your Body

For centuries it was believed that memory resided in the brain. Today neurophysiologists are challenging that assumption. *In reality, nobody knows for sure where the function of memory resides.*

What is *known* is that memory is diffused. Studies in the end of the nineteenth century supported the theory that the brain consists of a collection of highly specialized functional units which control, for example, speech, movement, and vision. Yet today, this doctrine of "localization and function" is hotly disputed.

While some memory does seem to be traced to the different zones of the cortex corresponding to the different senses and motor functions, neurophysiologists can't explain away the results of tests that go against this doctrine.

## The Holographic Brain

To determine the physical location of the memory trace, experiments were done on over 2,000 monkeys. The monkeys were first trained to do simple tasks. After the tasks had been learned, scientists removed different portions of the monkeys' brains. *Yet, regardless of the part of the brain removed, the monkeys were still able to perform the functions.*

Similar results have been found in brain damaged patients who have injured the part of their brain that was generally recognized to control writing or speaking. Yet, despite the injury (or removal) of the localized part of the brain that was to control a specific function, the patient was still able to perform that function to some degree. *Clearly the memory is being stored elsewhere, but where?*

Again, "memory is diffused." But diffused where? First of all, it appears to be diffused throughout the entire brain in such a way that *any part of the brain can restructure the whole memory*. This is known as the "holographic brain theory." Discovered by psychologist Karl Pribram in the mid-1960s, it draws on the analogy of holograms (those laser-generated pictures that can be viewed from all angles as if they were three-dimensional objects) to explain how memory is stored.

The nature of a hologram is such that it allows you to cut out any part of it and still see the entire 3-D image. Therefore, applying this theory to the brain, if the brain operates as a holographic plate, *any part of it reconstructs the whole*. Thus the function of your memory of how to speak, for example, is not relegated to one specialized functional unit in the brain, but rather represented by patterns throughout the brain operating like holograms to represent memory traces. That would explain the lack of memory loss in the monkeys' damaged brains, as well as with brain damaged patients.

Memory, therefore appears to be diffused throughout the brain in networks of holograms. But, is it the only place memory resides? *For memory is, first of all, a biological phenomenon with its roots in the senses.* You come to know your environment through your senses. And your senses take in information throughout your body.

## Locking in Memories with Your Senses

You have several types of memories—visual, verbal, olfactory or smell, tactile or touch, taste, and kinesthetic, or, of the muscles. The chemistry of memory is the activity of nerve cells, or neurons, communicating among themselves and the brain. These neurons are all over every inch of your body. The messengers themselves are specialized molecules called neurotransmitters.

Scientific research has shown that your neuronal activity has the ability to sift, choose, cultivate and eliminate memory. In other words, *cells throughout the body have memory*. How else could new cells be reproduced to replace new skin for healing if the body did not possess the memory of how to grow new cells?

Cell memory is the basis behind immunizations, which give the child a small dose of a disease for the purpose of creating the right type and amount of anti-bodies necessary for fighting off the disease <u>at the time of inoculation and for the rest of the child's life</u>. Should the disease enter the body again, the body remembers what type of anti-bodies to produce and in what amount. Just as we can accept that these cells have a memory function in performing their task, we can also accept the notion of other cells in our body having a memory too.

The ramification of this point is that you can use not only your left and your right brain, but your whole body to explore your power of memory. You have a holographic architecture of memory throughout your entire body that is dynamic in nature, constantly in motion, constantly reaching out across the information highways in your mind <u>and</u> in your body.

What's required is a holistic approach to accessing your memory. Through your intellectual *memory* you will learn how to engage your left brain for verbal processing and the right brain for visual image processing. You will also learn how to engage your body through *emotional memory*. This is accomplished by using all of your senses and bringing in your feelings to play with the information. In so doing you will be able to categorize it, find a pattern to it, see how it connects with what you already know, forming a network of holograms *spanning not only across your left and right brain but spanning a network throughout your entire body to include the information coming in from all your senses.*

This is the key strategy in developing your photographic mind. There are two primary advantages of this process:

- By connecting to the information through your emotions and various senses (and not just intellectual activity of your left and right brain) you will generate many access paths to trigger the recall of information.
- By connecting to the information through your emotions and senses you create an *emotional* bond with that information—a bond which gives you ownership of the information.

This emotional bond is the answer to overcoming the ineffectiveness of rote memorization. For as explained earlier, rote memorization is not effective because it doesn't include you in the picture. In contrast, reconnecting to the information through your intellectual memory (by picturing yourself physically involved with the information) does include you. And even better, the process of adding emotional attachment creates a bond that seals in the memory. It's through your emotional memory you take ownership of the information. In other words, suddenly it becomes your stuff. And study after study has shown that we do not forget that which we create.

## The Key to Learning and Memory: Involvement

A survey from the National Institute for Development and Administration at the University of Texas showed that we remember:

- 10% of what we read
- 20% of what we hear
- 30% of what we see
- 50% of what we see and hear
- 60% of what we say
- 90% of what we do and say

Why? Because by *doing* and *saying* we are involving ourselves, putting ourselves into the picture and taking ownership of whatever it is we are saying and doing—in other words, we are acting as a creator of knowledge instead of a consumer. Through this process we are performing as an active participant rather than a spectator on the sidelines.

Think how fantastic it would be if you retained 90% of what you learned—instead of the mere 10%, or 20% or 30% that most people take in. And then, taking this one step further, think of how easy it would be for you—*because you have this information readily available in your mind already*—think how you could play with it and apply this information to not only solve problems, but to rearrange this information to make new discoveries and connections that your peers can't even comprehend.

When this happens, your peers are no longer your peers. You are light-years ahead of them. Why? Because you aren't preoccupied with handling the information overload. You are just doing it—*using your left brain, right brain and body in a holistic approach to take in information and stimuli from your environment in such a way that you can easily reconnect with it when you need to.*

Suddenly it is all your stuff. And it became yours when you saw how it fit into your world. When you created the connections that allowed you to make sense of the information in a way that was significant to you—allowing you to remember the information perfectly clearly when you needed to recall it.

This is not an act of memory—it's an act of reconnecting to the information. And the four memory processes presented in this book will enable your mind to speed ahead into a realm that your peers don't have time to play in because they are too busy trying to burn the information into their brain. REPEAT—REPEAT—REPEAT those names and numbers. REPEAT—REPEAT—REPEAT the sales presentation until it's perfect. REPEAT—REPEAT—REPEAT the "Things-To-Do" lists.

You, on the other hand, will be using your left brain, your right brain and your body to connect with that same information in a meaningful, yet playful manner, that will let you record, retain, and retrieve the data easily and effortlessly.

This is what the four powerful memory systems in this course will allow you to do. But before you start to work with these systems, let's take a Memory Assessment Test to get a baseline on your memory skill as of this moment.

## Memory Assessment Exercise

How many words can you recall from a group of 20? Let's find out shall we, and get a baseline of your memory ability. Spend the next 60 seconds looking at the 20 words that follow and then write as many as you can (in any order) on the lines below. Use your other hand to cover up the original list. *This is not a test of your potential, this is a test of your ability today.* So relax and use any technique to help you recall the words.

NEST, SNAKE, STAR, CONDOM, SAMPAN, NAIL, ACCELERATE, PENCIL, RAPIST, MONEY, MATURE, PONTIFICATE, SKUNK, THING-A-MAJIG, DULL, DENTIST, CAR, BREASTS, LEMON, HAWAII.

**Your Answers**

1. _____
2. _____
3. _____
4. _____
5. _____
6. _____
7. _____
8. _____
9. _____
10. _____
11. _____
12. _____
13. _____
14. _____
15. _____
16. _____
17. _____
18. _____
19. _____
20. _____

Now compare your list to the original 20 words and write the number that you correctly recalled in the space below.

Your Total Score: _____

## Memory Traces Are Not Born Equal

People who take this Memory Assessment before working with the memory systems in this book remember on average five to seven words. *However, the number of words you remembered is not the significance of this test.* The purpose of this test is to see which specific words you did recall.

As you will soon see, memory traces are not born equal. If they were, you would have been able to remember all the words with the same degree of effort. But you didn't. And here's why:

• **One reason, as you learned earlier, is that concrete words are easier to recall than abstract verbal information.** This is due to the fact that abstract verbal words are difficult to picture, therefore they are only retained by your verbal left brain. In other words they don't have the *dual representation* of concrete items—which can be seen by both the visual right brain and the verbal left brain.

So most likely, you did not recall the abstract words of ACCELERATE, PONTIFICATE, DULL and MATURE.

• **Another reason is that the mind doesn't easily remember things it doesn't understand and hence can't categorize**—which is also why the word PONTIFICATE is often left out. A second word that falls into this category of "not being understood" is SAMPAN, meaning a small boat of the Far East. If you didn't know what it was, you couldn't categorize it and therefore reduced the likelihood of you remembering it.

While these two reasons of "abstract information" and "inability to categorize" explain why you didn't remember some of the words, there are probably still more words you forgot that don't fall into either of these two categories.

Most people also don't remember the words PENCIL or NEST or NAIL. Yet these are not abstract verbal information, nor are they items you can't categorize. The reason these words aren't often recalled in this exercise is because they aren't emotionally charged with meaning and hence don't elicit an emotional response.

Now, let's take a look at the words most people remember from this list. They are CONDOM, RAPIST, BREASTS, SKUNK, MONEY, THING-A-MAJIG and HAWAII. These words have the highest recall from this test because they elicit strong emotions.

The emotion can be either positive or negative. It doesn't matter. The importance is not in the *type* of emotion, but the *degree* of the emotion. Why is this so critical to memory? Because emotion sorts out what is important to you— an event that has touched you emotionally is recorded with more depth of processing and elaboration and it leaves the deepest mark in your memory.

*Just as your imagination vividly conjures up a picture to aid in recall, emotion deeply engraves that which you want to remember*. Imagination and emotion are your two biggest allies in your ability to remember.

---

### Flashbacks with Feeling

The impact of emotions on the memory process is easy to see when you analyze your own memory. *Don't you dwell mostly on what moved you, shook you, rattled you, shocked you, pleased you, or annoyed you?*

- You can easily recall the unpleasant situations in your life. Take a minute now to bring a few of these up.
- Now, think about the happy times in your life.

Both of these types of experiences are easy to recall because, good or bad, they made an impact on you. You felt them. You were stirred by them. They affected you. Affect—that's a-f-f-e-c-t as in affection, as in feeling, as in emotion.

---

The reason you can easily remember highly emotional experiences is because you are using your whole body to remember them. The concept is that memory is a function of the whole brain, *but it is first of all a biological phenomenon with its roots in the senses*—visual, verbal, olfactory (or smell), tactile (or touch and taste), and kinesthetic (or of the muscles).

Again you have not only <u>intellect memory</u>—referring to ideas that can be expressed by words and pictures—but <u>emotional memory</u> as well, referring to impressions that can be expressed by feelings—*feelings that cannot always be put into words.*

## The Anatomy of a Memory

Scientists probing the memory process discovered that the chemistry of memory is the activity of nerve cells, or neurons, communicating among themselves and the brain. These neurons are all over every inch of your body. The messengers themselves are specialized molecules called neurotransmitters. As stated before, neuronal activity has the ability to sift, choose, cultivate and eliminate memory traces.

The art of memory resides in organizing the storage of traces so these traces will be easy to access. Again, the impetus behind this is the eternal quest of your mind and your body, constantly seeking to make sense out of data or stimuli received from your environment through your senses, by developing patterns or categories in your mind and cross-referencing one category to another.

Now let's look at how the emotional process works. You first classify into categories what you perceive in a sensory mode—sight, hearing, smell, etc. These categories then proceed to *affective* categories—which are your emotions—and then to the intellectual memory, where you make a verbal judgement on the information. This is holistic memory—*emotional memory encompassing the body and intellectual memory encompassing the left and right brain.*

In other words, just as using your visual right brain improves the ability of your verbal left brain to remember, using your whole body to aid in recall improves your ability to remember even more dramatically. And how do you record memories with your body? By using your senses. *The rule here is the more senses you record something with, the easier it will be to retrieve.* You can improve the recording of memories by becoming more aware of feelings and by developing better observation skills, which will in turn enable you to better categorize the information, thus engraving the information into both emotional and intellectual memories.

This again, is the basis of the memory systems in this book: left brain, right brain and body. It is a holistic process that expands on the natural memory processes that your mind and body already use.

## Reconnecting to Your Memories

Earlier you learned the difference between *reconnecting* versus *memorizing*. This concept takes on even greater meaning now that you know about the importance of emotions in improving your memory.

The act of *memorizing by rote* requires you to hold something up in an empty vacuum state and REPEAT—REPEAT—REPEAT until it is burned into your mind. In other words, it leaves you out of the picture. Reconnecting, however, puts you in the picture by involving your visual right brain to conjure up a vivid mental image through imagination. By adding the emotional aspect you are *involving yourself in the memory, you are feeling something* and it is those feelings, *fueled by emotion*, that are ingraining the memory into your body— recording it deeply by categorizing it, cross-referencing it, creating your own connections so that you can reconnect with it and retrieve it on a moment's notice.

The ramification of all this is the reason why rote memorization is not effective is because it is boring—and it is both boring and ineffective because it leaves you out. If you are being left out, your mind is not engaged in the material. You are just viewing it over and over.

Again, studies show that we remember 10% of what we read, 20% of what we hear, 30% of what we see, 50% of what we see and hear, 60% of what we say and 90% of what we do and say. The very nature of using your whole brain and body in the memory process means you are creating ownership of the material and developing networks by which you can reconnect with that material again.

Now, relating all this to the Memory Assessment, the reason you were able to remember some words better than others is that some *were charged with feelings for you*. This is your emotional memory at work.

## The Process of Memory

What is the stuff memories are made of? *First of all, memory is thought—involving words and numbers. It is also visual images involving imagination. Plus it is feelings and moods involving emotion.* Memory is your <u>whole</u> self. You possess a *holistic* memory. And once trained, your memory is so unbelievably powerful because it taps into the natural ability of your *whole body* to remember. Not just your verbal left brain—*not even just your visual right brain*—but with your whole body through the senses as they encode data and stimuli from your environment.

In both animals and human beings, sensory information through sight, sound, smell, touch and taste is initially processed in what is called the *primary sensory areas* of the brain. The information is then relayed to neighboring brain regions know as *memory maps*. It then leaves the memory maps and goes to the *limbic system* of the brain.

What is the limbic system? The limbic system is part of the so-called "old brain" or "lower brain." It is responsible for activating emotional responses such as fight or flight and sexual desires. The limbic system is the physiological "Ground Zero" of our emotions. Our emotions spring forth from the limbic system automatically. We don't need to think about triggering ourselves to feel hunger, to feel fear, to feel love—we just do—and that is the function of the limbic system: to help insure our survival by triggering these feelings. And in serving this function of triggering the responses to help insure our survival, the limbic system is also believed to trigger the function of memory. How? By sealing in emotions.

This function of the limbic system was first described by Sigmond Freud in the late 1800s and is widely accepted by neuropsychologists today. The theory is one which we began this book with: that life would be impossible if you didn't have the ability to remember at all—for it would be as if you were doing everything for the first time. In other words, you could not survive without memory.

Again, the limbic system helps insure our survival by triggering us to feel hunger, feel fear, feel love. It also helps us survive by triggering emotions that will recall our experiences. In other words, by using the emotions springing forth from your limbic system, the memory process is insuring your survival by arming you with the knowledge of past experience in the form of memories that allow you to make sense of your current reality.

## Emotions Organize Memories

How does emotion seal in memory? By organizing our thoughts and actions. The ability of emotions to organize thoughts is so crucial in the first place *because, as you have already learned, of the three stages of record, retain and retrieve, it is the third stage of retrieval that causes us the most memory problems.* And why? Because of a lack of organization of the memories that were recorded and retained.

Just as the files need to be organized in your file cabinet for rapid retrieval, so too do memories need to be organized in your mind and your body. The way to do this is through emotions. Study after study has shown that people can dramatically improve their memory by becoming aware of feelings through their senses and by developing better observation skills. This in turn boosts the ability to file and categorize the information, thus engraving the information into both the emotional and intellectual memories.

## Scoring Your Emotional Memory

Looking back at the Memory Assessment you did earlier, you can see for yourself how emotional memory fits into the picture. You already discovered that the words you were most likely to forget were ACCELERATE, PONTIFICATE, DULL, MATURE and SAMPAN. Why? Because these words are either abstract verbal information or hard to understand, thus making them too difficult to categorize.

Yet most people don't remember the words PENCIL, NEST, NAIL, DENTIST, or CAR either. They are concrete words, so yes, they are easy to picture. But to the average individual, they do not elicit strong emotions unless—*and this is the key*—unless you own a special <u>pencil</u>, or had to pay a huge bill for the exterminator to get a <u>nest</u> of wasps out from under your gutter, or have a hang nail that hurts, or personally have a fear of <u>dentists</u>, or recently got in a <u>car</u> wreck or bought a new <u>car</u>. Unless you had an emotional connection to these rather boring words, then you most likely didn't remember these words while you did remember CONDOM, RAPIST, MONEY, SKUNK, BREASTS, HAWAII and THING-A-MA-JIG.

That leaves just three more words—LEMON, SNAKE and STAR. People who remember more than 7 words usually remember these three as well, while people who had a hard time remembering CONDOM, RAPIST, MONEY, SKUNK, BREASTS, HAWAII, and THINK-A-MA-JIG, usually forgot LEMON, SNAKE and STAR.

Again, the specific words you recalled may differ from those which are generally the ones most frequently remembered. The reason is because what makes the average person feel anger, shock, fear, or excitement may not necessarily cause the same reaction in you. This is similar to the fact that two people who see the same movie, read the same book, or see the same accident do not necessarily remember the same things. And why is this so? The answer is because your perceptions are to some degree your own creations. *It is not fixed images we rely on when recalling a memory but recreations and imaginations, or the past molded in ways appropriate for the present.*

---

## The False Hopes of Eidetic Imagery

There is a difference between a *true photographic memory* and the *photographic mind* you will be developing through the workshops of this book. A photographic mind is much more powerful than a photographic memory—a phenomenon which psychologists call "eidetic imagery."

Eidetic means identical or duplicative. Eidetic imagery is a very strong after-image than enables a person to duplicate the picture mentally and describe it in detail shortly after looking at it. Eidetic imagery is very rare— only 5% to 10% of children have it and extremely few adults. Adults who do have it are, more often than not, the so-called *idiot-savants* who display a genius-like ability in one area (such as in performing mathematical equations in their mind), yet have a very low overall IQ.

Eidetic imagery differs from the popular notion of a "photographic mind" in several ways:

- The image fades soon after viewing the scene or document. It does not stay with the person over a prolonged period of time, lasting only for a few seconds to a few minutes.
- This image is affected by the subjective state of the viewer, meaning that it may contain additions, omissions, distortions—with the aspects of the scene or document that are of most interest to the person being produced in the most detail.
- The eidetic image cannot be brought back after it has faded away. This ability is a function of short-term memory and cannot be used to improve long-term memory.

While, on the surface, eidetic memory sounds wonderful, the nature of this ability appears to be of little value for the true purpose of memory. On the other hand, the popular notion of a photographic mind as applied in this course **does** give you the ability to improve your long-term memory. And, as stated early on, this ability is a *learned behavior or trainable skill, rather than the innate ability of eidetic imagery.*

The world is constantly changing. Therefore we must be able to react to it not in terms of what was previously stored (as fixed images that are no longer part of our surroundings), but in a way that will adapt to the new and unexpected, while acknowledging our individual past experiences.

The photographic mind you will gain from this course allows you to play with the information and stimuli you are taking in through your senses so that it becomes useful to you as you cope with your environment.

## A Photographic Mind is a Flexible Mind

While memory gives us the knowledge we need to survive (without it, we would view every situation as a new experience) it also gives us the ultimate tool for success—to predict the likelihood of a future event based on patterns recorded, retained and retrieved from the past.

Again, this is the purpose of our limbic system—our lower brain—to ensure our survival needs are met. The limbic system is responsible for the memory process, and the vehicle it uses as a catalyst is emotion. The role of emotion is to capture your memories through your senses in the recording stage, and then seal in and organize these memories into categories in the retaining stage so that they can be easily accessed in the retrieval stage.

Through this process your memory categorizes information and stimuli from your environment in such a way as to enable you to retrieve this information quickly. In performing this function your memory allows you to react appropriately to the continually changing environment of the present through your judgments, values and interests arrived at from past experiences.

The importance of all this becomes clear when you understand that the brain categorizes stimuli in accordance with *past experiences* and *present need and desires*. This categorization constitutes the basis of perception and recognition—meaning that through our encounters with the environment we try various ways of categorizing stimuli, and those that lead to meaningful or useful behavior will be reinforced.

For example, how can you recognize a face that has grown old—a friend that you haven't see for 10 years—if you are searching for a fixed image of their younger looking face? You couldn't. You need to give that image some flexibility, don't you? And you do. How? You do it by not relying on *fixed images, but categories* that allow you to recreate the face. Again, *memory is the past molded in ways appropriate for the present.*

Here is another example. People who know only the slightest knowledge of art can differentiate between two impressionists painters. And too, someone who is familiar with the art of Picasso can differentiate originals from adept imitations. Similarly, when you are familiar with an artist's music, you can easily identify a new song of theirs, even though you have never heard it before. You could also recognize recent day photographs of areas you visited ten years prior. And why is this possible? *Because it is not fixed images you rely on but recreations*—recreations of similar <u>patterns</u>—be it the patterns of musical notes in a song or the patterns of landscape in the photos.

When we recognize these things we are doing more than recalling the past, we are categorizing—our recognition of a painting or a person is the recognition of a category, not of a specific item. People are never exactly the same as they were moments before, and objects are never seen in exactly the same way. Our capacity to remember is not for specific recall of a stored image. Rather, it is an ability to organize the world around us into categories—some general, some specific. And the resource we use to categorize is the resource of our emotion.

When you speak of a stored mental image of a friend, which image are you referring to? Even factual information—such as phone numbers—we remember specifically and categorically at the same time—a specific phone number to a category of our friend's image.

Again, the reason our memory works this way is for survival: we need not only stored images but procedures that will help us understand the world. And again, the reason is simply this: *your mind wants to know why—your mind is constantly seeking to make sense out of things by developing patterns or categories and cross-referencing one category to another.* This is the purpose of memory—to take specifics and break them down into categories of information that will allow for meaningful application to your changing world.

*We simply do not store images or bits, but become more richly endowed with the capacity to categorize in connected ways.* Human intelligence is not just knowing more, but reworking, recategorizing, and thus putting information together in new and novel ways.

The environment doesn't teach you what you should know: you need to make your own sense of the environment through the categorization of incoming stimuli through your senses. The more observant you are with your senses, the greater your chances of capturing your observations on more than one memory map. The more memory maps your observations are captured on, the stronger the trace, and the greater the recall because the more avenues of access you are leaving. Again, the better the storage, the better the recall.

## Overcoming Memory Blocks with Emotion

Memory is an amazing process. Through the care and research of Alzheimer's patients, psychologists and neuropsychologists are learning far more about the dynamics of memory. The benefit to all of us is great as we learn to unlock the secrets to memory in our own every day life. And the key element always comes back to emotions.

Earlier you learned that a breakdown in memory can occur in any of the three stages of memory—recording, retaining and retrieval. Now let's review those reasons and see why the ultimate cause for each breakdown is emotion.

• **In the recording stage** the breakdown is most likely to be a lack of attention (absent-mindedness) or distortion.

- Absent-mindedness is simply caused by a lack of observation, or in other words it is *a situation where you are not using your senses to capture information.* Emotional memory of the body enters through your senses. Therefore when you are absent-minded, you are not using your senses to record a memory and therefore emotional memory, or a lack of it, is the cause for this breakdown.
- Distortion means that you remember things the way you want to remember them—your record is *affected* by your own *values and feelings.* Feelings are emotions.

• **In the second stage of retaining** the reason for the breakdown is due either to decay or repression. *Again, emotion is the basis of both of these breakdowns.*

- Decay occurs when you are removed from the memory and it becomes void of emotions.

- Repression occurs when you emotionally can't deal with the memory ever happening in the first place.

• **The last stage of memory is retrieval.** This is the stage where the majority of problems occur because you simply can't find the information. You can't locate the memory trace. And, recalling the analogy with the file cabinet, the reason you can't locate it is because the information wasn't stored in an organized manner.

Simply opening the drawer and putting in a file doesn't mean you will be able to find the file when you need it. You need to organize the files. So how do you organize memories? *Through categories that are put onto memory maps generated by the neurons receiving the information through your senses.* In other words, you categorize the memories through emotion.

Emotion, resulting from the incoming data and stimuli from your senses and creating activity through your limbic system, is the key to memory. The evidence is there in looking at the types of information we easily remember and in the type of information we easily forget.

Earlier you learned about the three types of long-term memory—procedural, involved in learning a skill (such as typing or tying your shoes), episodic, referring to personal events such as birthday parties, and semantic memory, which is the learning of factual information. You discovered that the easiest memories for you to recall are personal events and skills. And the hardest was *semantic—the learning of factual information.*

As mentioned before, semantic information is the one type of information that doesn't have a connection to time or place—meaning you don't remember when or where you learned the information. The reason semantic information is so hard to remember is that it is void of emotion. You weren't involved with the information as you learned it, you just held it up and said REPEAT—REPEAT—REPEAT to burn it into your brain.

*The key to boosting your memory power then, is using both emotional memory and intellectual memory.* Memory is a learned skill and this applies to both your intellectual and emotional memories. You can train your intellectual memory and you can train your emotional memory. This is the holistic approach. And that is exactly what the four memory systems in this course will show you how to do.

These systems are simple to learn because they work with your natural abilities. But please, once you learn them, don't think you've got it down and pull yourself back. You need to be an active participant in this program. You need to create ownership of these processes. Remember the statistics we discussed earlier:

- If you limit your participation to reading this course you will likely remember only 20%.
- If you are an *active learner, saying and doing the activities and exercises* you can retain 90% of this course *the first time you go through it.*

## Are You Ready to Begin?

Your memory is a wonderful gift. Through the workshops that follow you will learn how to celebrate its power. Enjoy it and have fun with the interactive exercises. Above all, be prepared to be surprised at the incredible power of the photographic mind that will soon be at your command.

# PART II
# The Four Memory Systems

# The Link System

The opening chapters introduced you to the holistic approach of *The Photographic Mind* system which provided some background on how you can boost your memory power up to 500%. This is accomplished by tapping into the intellectual memory of your mind and the emotional memory of your body. You are now ready to put this concept to work for you with the Link System, which is the first of the four memory systems you'll be taught.

The Link System is fun and easy to learn, but best of all it is very effective for memorizing the many lists of items you make for yourself everyday—from "To Do" lists to grocery lists.

## The Two Phases of the Link System

This memory system consists of two phases. In Phase 1 you form a mental picture for each item in the list, using your right brain and your resource of imagination. In Phase 2 you link, or chain, the items together in a crazy, illogical, bizarre story and use emotion to lock in the memory.

What you are doing is making a connection between two unrelated items with a ridiculous picture that associates the items together and causes you to feel an emotional response to what is going on in the picture. Once you've linked "item 1" to "item 2" you can link "item 2" to "item 3" and so on all through your list. This is called a "link story" because it tells how each item is linked to, or leads to the next.

Just as a flip book animates a series of still cartoon drawings with the simple action of your thumb flipping through the pages, your mind animates these static images as it reels through the link story in your "mind's eye." Using the Link System you create a library of flip books that you can speed read in seconds.

## Jump Start Your Memory with Mental Flip Books

For example, imagine you are going to the store to buy:

eggs

bacon

milk

bread

lemon

By linking the five items together in a crazy, illogical, bizarre story (and locking it in with emotion) you could create the following mental flip book:

*Hundreds of eggs being pulled on sleds of sizzling bacon down a mountain slope of frozen milk.*

*At the bottom there is a ski lodge made of gigantic pieces of crumbling bread.*

*The crumbling bread cascades into a chair lift car which is a humongous lemon—and you are in it, teetering on the brink of disaster.*

As you can see, each item in the link takes you directly to the next item. To recall this list you simply begin with the first scene in your flip book and mentally run through it until the end. The list of items will be easy to remember as you proceed because each item leads you to the next.

The reason this system is so powerful, as you learned earlier, is because the mind thinks in pictures. *But remember, you need to make a crazy, illogical, bizarre picture.* The rule here is no boring pictures. You need to vividly see the item in such a ludicrous and bizarre manner that it's impossible to forget. Let your imagination run wild and use your emotions to seal in the memory. Your imagination and emotion are your best allies in boosting your memory power.

Creating mental flip books is fun and easy. Here are five ways to jump start your storyboard:

    1. Inject action into your picture.

    2. Use exaggeration by making the items bigger than life.

3. Increase the quantity of the item.

4. Include yourself in the picture (in an illogical or bizarre way).

5. Be sure to use emotion by involving your senses.

## Applying the 5 Guidelines for Mental Flip Books

Using the previous link story, let's see how each of these five guidelines were used to create the links in the above flip book.

The first guideline is to inject action. Just look at all the scenes involving action—*sledding bacon, crumbling bread, teetering lemon.*

The second guideline is to use exaggeration by making the items bigger than life. This was used in creating the scenes for the *gigantic pieces of bread and humongous lemon.*

The third guideline is to increase the item quantity, as with *hundreds* of eggs.

The fourth guideline was to include yourself in the picture, as shown by the scene in which you *put yourself in the lemon chair lift.*

And the fifth guideline is to use emotion, such as the *emotion of fear*, as you are about to fall out of the lemon chair lift.

There are two reasons why making these pictures in a ridiculous manner will enable you to recall the items. First of all, this process engages your imagination by creating a crazy, illogical, bizarre image of the item. And earlier you read that the mind simply remembers better what it creates on its own. Secondly, these crazy, illogical, bizarre pictures make a deeper trace in your memory by eliciting your emotions such as laughter, shock, or fear. And again, as you read in Part I, we remember most what shocks us, moves us, or stirs our soul. This is the secret of your emotional memory at work for you.

---

### A Visualization Exercise

To demonstrate how vividly you need to see your picture, let's go through a mental exercise to visualize a lemon. For this demonstration, don't picture the lemon as it was used in the story (as a chair lift). Instead, picture it as a real lemon in your kitchen.

Pick it up. Look at it. Feel the dimpled texture. See the bright yellow, shiny skin. Now putting it down onto a cutting board, pick up a sharp knife and cut the lemon in half. Feel the knife pierce the skin and slice through the fruit. Hold up one of the halves to your nose and smell the clean citric scent. Then squeeze the lemon and feel the juices run down into your hand. Now, bite into the lemon.

*If you are vividly imagining this picture you should have a mouth full of saliva by now.* Why? Are you actually biting into the lemon? No, but research has shown that the body has difficulty telling the difference between a real and a vividly imagined picture. When you actually see that lemon, your eye sends an electrical signal to the vision center in your brain. And when you vividly imagine that lemon in your *mind's eye* it activates the same electrical signals.

The key to making the Link System work is to use this power of visualization to conjure up crazy, illogical, bizarre mental scenes in a mental flip book and then elicit emotions to lock these images into memory.

---

## Take the Grocery List Pretest

Your first *Photographic Mind Workshop* shows you how to use the Link System to remember items on a grocery list. But before you participate in the workshop, let's take a pretest to see how many of these items you can easily recall without using the Link System.

There are 21 items on the list. You've already heard the first five in the sample link story. The following list repeats those first five items and then adds 16 more. *Don't try to come up with links just yet.* <u>This is just a pretest</u>. After you've read the list, cover it up and write as many items as you can remember.

## • Grocery List Pretest

Eggs, bacon, milk, bread, lemon, cottage cheese, salad dressing, spaghetti, chicken, diapers, fish, lamb, Cheerios, hot dogs, bananas, pretzels, T-bone steak, black olives, potato chips, rice, oranges.

Now cover up the list above and write below as many as you can remember.

1. _____
2. _____
3. _____
4. _____
5. _____
6. _____
7. _____
8. _____
9. _____
10. _____
11. _____
12. _____
13. _____
14. _____
15. _____
16. _____
17. _____
18. _____
19. _____
20. _____
21. _____

Check your answers to the original list. Write the total number of correct answers below.

Your Total Score: _____

Now let's analyze your score. You probably remembered most or all of the first five that we have already linked into a story—eggs, bacon, milk, bread and lemon. How many others did you remember? The goal is for you to remember ALL of them. At the end of the upcoming *Photographic Mind Workshop* you will retake the test and I think you will be amazed at your newfound ability to *recall not only the items*, but the *exact order* as well. When you're ready let's begin the first workshop.

## Photographic Mind Workshop: To Market, To Market

### Step 1: Active Learning Session

To enhance your experience of the material please play the *Accelerated Learning Music* soundtrack (located on Track #2 of your *Brain Supercharger* CD) while you complete the following workshop exercise.

You are now ready to learn how to apply the Link System through the three-step process that will be used throughout this book. Step 1 is the Active Learning Session. In this session you'll participate in an interactive learning process by reading, seeing, and verbalizing—*out loud*—the material you wish to recall.

The following link story describes the mental flip book that will let you remember your grocery list with ease. The use of visual icons have been incorporated into the workshop to help you chunk and visualize the information. They are provided only as mental references, and not necessarily the images you would conjure up in your imagination. Normally you would create your own (much more powerful) mental imagery in your "mind's eye" using the powers of your imagination. As you read along, let your imagination play with the crazy, illogical, bizarre pictures and use your emotions to lock these into memory.

*Hundreds of **eggs** are being pulled on sleds of sizzling **bacon** down a mountain*

*slope of frozen* **milk**. *At the bottom there is a ski lodge made of gigantic pieces*

*of crumbling* **bread**. *The crumbling bread cascades into a chair lift car made*

*out of a humongous* **lemon** *and you are in it, teetering on the brink of disaster.*

*You and the lemon slide down into a container of curdled* **cottage cheese**. *In the*

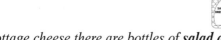

*cottage cheese there are bottles of* **salad dressing** *floating around. You grab onto*

*a bottle while someone throws you a huge rope of* **spaghetti**. *Tied to the other end*

*of the spaghetti is a* **chicken** *wearing dirty* **diapers** *and squashing out of the*

*dirty diapers are hundreds of little* **fish**. *Each fish is wearing a* **lamb***skin coat with*

**Cheerios** *for buttons. The Cheerios are being eaten by hungry* **hot dogs** *that are*

*ridden by bunches of* **bananas** *who are throwing lassos made of* **pretzels**. *The*

*pretzels lasso a* **T-Bone** *steak smothered with hundreds of* **black olives** *dropping* *from above out of a flying **potato chip** being piloted through puffy clouds*

*of **rice** by a smiling Florida **orange**. The smiling Florida orange crashes into*

*the eggs at the top of the mountain and breaks every one of them.*

Were you able to see the pictures with vivid detail? *What kind of bread did you see—was it white bread, rye bread or whole wheat? What did the cottage cheese container look like—whose label was it? And what about the potato chip—did it have ridges, was it barbecued flavor, or just plain?* These are the kinds of details you should be calling upon your imagination to supply. *Did you use all of your senses to record what was going on? Could you smell the curdled cottage cheese and feel the disgust of the dirty diapers squashing out the fish? Let those emotions come into play.* The more you do, the easier and faster your recall will be.

You are going to read this story again. This time, be sure to vividly see all the events and the grocery items in this story. Your mind already thinks in pictures, all you need is to supply the detail to bring each picture alive. See the colors, smell the smells, feel the action going on. This time, when you read the story, really focus on bringing the scenes to life and let your emotions come into play.

*Hundreds of **eggs** are being pulled on sleds of sizzling **bacon** down a mountain*

*slope of frozen **milk**. At the bottom there is a ski lodge made of gigantic pieces*

*of crumbling **bread**. The crumbling bread cascades into a chair lift car made*

*out of a humongous **lemon** and you are in it, teetering on the brink of disaster.*

*You and the lemon slide down into a container of curdled **cottage cheese**. In the*

*cottage cheese there are bottles of **salad dressing** floating around. You grab onto*

*a bottle while someone throws you a huge rope of **spaghetti**. Tied to the other end*

*of the spaghetti is a **chicken** wearing dirty **diapers** and squashing out of the*

*dirty diapers are hundreds of little **fish**. Each fish is wearing a **lamb**skin coat with*

***Cheerios** for buttons. The Cheerios are being eaten by hungry **hot dogs** that are*

*ridden by bunches of **bananas** who are throwing lassos made of **pretzels**. The*

*pretzels lasso a **T-Bone** steak smothered with hundreds of **black olives** dropping*

*from above out of a flying **potato chip** being piloted through puffy clouds*

*of **rice** by a smiling Florida **orange**. The smiling Florida orange crashes into*

*the eggs at the top of the mountain and breaks every one of them.*

Did the pictures become more clearer to you this time? Could you visualize in greater detail and at a faster pace? You have only read this story two times now, but already you may be mentally jumping ahead, seeing the next scene in your mental flip book. This is easy for you to do because your mind naturally thinks in pictures. It uses your imagination to conjure up these crazy, illogical, bizarre images and it uses your emotions to lock in those pictures—and best of all, it has fun doing it.

This is the difference between "rote memorization" of the list and "reconnecting" to the list through your intellectual and emotional memory that you read about earlier in the book. You can see how you are becoming involved with this list of items, rather than holding them up and saying REPEAT—REPEAT—REPEAT until you burn them into your brain. *Rote memorization is hard, boring and ineffective because it doesn't involve you. Holistic memory is fun, easy and effective because it puts you in the picture.*

## Chunking the Flip Book

To help you recall the mental flip book, let's break the story into link phrases, or chunks of information. As you read in Part I, chunking is a way to help you break the whole down into manageable parts. In addition, let's increase your involvement by having you recite each link phrase as you see it. Verbalizing is a very powerful way to aid your recall.

Earlier you read the statistics which stated we remember 10% of what we read, 20% of what we hear, 30% of what we see, 50% of what we see and hear, 60% of what we say and 90% of what we do and say. *By saying this story out loud and mentally "doing it," or going through it vividly in your mind's eye, you will greatly improve the record it makes on your memory so that you can retain it and retrieve it easily and quickly.*

Please recite (out loud), the following chunked word phrases. As you do, focus in your mind's eye on your mental flip book.

Hundreds of **eggs** are being pulled on sleds of sizzling **bacon** down a mountain

slope of frozen **milk**. At the bottom there is a ski lodge made of gigantic pieces

of crumbling **bread**. The crumbling bread cascades into a chair lift car made

out of a humongous **lemon** and you are in it, teetering on the brink of disaster.

You and the lemon slide down into a container of curdled **cottage cheese**. In the

cottage cheese there are bottles of **salad dressing** floating around. You grab onto

a bottle while someone throws you a huge rope of **spaghetti**. Tied to the other end

of the spaghetti is a **chicken** wearing dirty **diapers** and squashing out of the

dirty diapers are hundreds of little **fish**. Each fish is wearing a **lamb**skin coat with

**Cheerios** for buttons. The Cheerios are being eaten by hungry **hot dogs** that are

ridden by bunches of **bananas** who are throwing lassos made of **pretzels**. The *pretzels lasso a **T-Bone** steak smothered with hundreds of **black olives** dropping*

*from above out of a flying **potato chip** being piloted through puffy clouds*

*of **rice** by a smiling Florida **orange**. The smiling Florida orange crashes into*

*the eggs at the top of the mountain and breaks every one of them.*

Now let's quickly review this flip book in your mind by answering the following questions:

> *What are the eggs sledding on?*
> *What is your chair lift made out of?*
> *What is squashing out of the dirty diapers?*
> *Who is wearing the dirty diapers?*
> *The bananas are riding on what?*
> *What is being lassoed? And, finally, what is piloting the*
>    *potato chip?*

If you have been vividly imaging these mental images, the answers to these questions should pop into your head. Why? *Because your mind thinks in pictures.* This is easy for your mind to do—much easier than staring at a piece of paper with 21 grocery list items on it saying REPEAT—REPEAT—REPEAT to every one.

Rote memory uses only your left brain. The Link System involves your left and right brain for intellectual memory plus your body for emotional memory. This allows you to leave many memory traces to reconnect you with the specific items in this story because you are engaging your whole body as you create the flip book in your memory factory.

## Step 2: Passive Learning Session

Now that you have chunked the comic strip in your mind's eye and verbaliz‌ the words for each link, you are ready to proceed to Step 2, the Passive Learn‌ng Session.

The link story you learned in the Active Learning Session is illustrated below without the use of any words. Spend the next two minutes gazing at the pictures. As this session is designed for unconscious learning, allowing your mind to wander will give you the maximum benefit. Try not to concentrate on any one illustration.

As you gaze at the images, feel your mind flip through the scenes. Let your right brain bring the animation to life with visual details and use your senses to lock in the images. See the colors, smell the smells, feel the action going on and let your emotions come into play. Just relax and let the whole scene replay effortlessly in your memory factory.

After spending a few minutes reviewing these images, you are ready to plug into the *Brain Supercharger* CD.

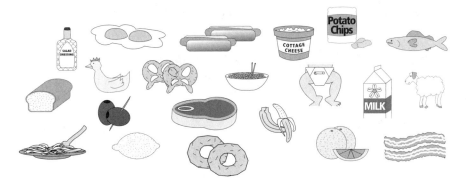

**To help lock-in your lesson please play the *Super Memory Transformation* Soundtrack (located on Track #3 of your *Brain Supercharger* CD). Put the book aside for now and make sure to use stereo headphones. Find a comfortable position & quiet place where you can rest undisturbed for the next 30 minutes.**

## You Think Faster Than You Speak or Write

During the time you spent looking at the images, you could have mentally run through the link story several times in your head—yet you could only have said it once, and not even had enough time to write it once. That's why training your memory is so important—*because you can think faster than you can speak or write*. By improving your memory you will free yourself from the time consuming process of writing notes to yourself or repeating over and over again to yourself the things you need to know.

This link story is now in your long-term memory. You could go to the store without your list and remember to buy every single item on that list. So let's try it! At the beginning of this lesson you took a Grocery List Pretest. Now it's time to take this test again in Step 3 and prove to yourself how you have boosted your memory with the easy and fun Link System.

## Step 3: Assessment

Your final step in this workshop is to test your recall of the grocery items. Simply visualize the link story in your mind by running through your mental flip book. As you do, write the 21 grocery list items in the spaces provided in order of their appearance in the story. Then compare your list to the answers and write your total score on the score line (each correct answer counts as one point).

### Grocery List Recall

1. _____
2. _____
3. _____
4. _____
5. _____
6. _____
7. _____
8. _____
9. _____
10. _____

11. _____

12. _____

13. _____

14. _____

15. _____

16. _____

17. _____

18. _____

19. _____

20. _____

21. _____

Your Total Score: _____

(Answers: 1. eggs 2. bacon 3. milk 4. bread 5. lemon 6. cottage cheese 7. salad dressing 8. spaghetti 9. chicken 10. diapers 11. fish 12. lamb 13. Cheerios 14. hot dogs 15. bananas 16. pretzels 17. T-bone steak 18. black olives 19. potato chips 20. rice 21. oranges)

Now, compare this list to your pretest and congratulate yourself at how much your ability to remember has improved in this short period of time. (Note: You need to score 19 or more to proceed. If your score is lower than that, please review Steps 1 and 2 and then retake the test.)

## A Simple Cure for Absent-mindedness

The Link System is just the first of four powerful memory systems presented in this book. It is very effective on memory tasks that require a listing of items in sequential order such as grocery lists or "To Do" lists.

You can also use the same 2-phase process of the Link System to cure absent-mindedness. For example, to use the Link to help you remember where you put your keys, simply:

1. Form a mental image of your keys and a mental image of the place you set them down.
2. Link the two images in a crazy, illogical bizarre image, and then seal in that image with emotion.

The following will illustrate the use of this process to recall putting your keys on the kitchen table. First, imagine your keys are heavy and huge, while the table is small and unstable. Secondly, see the table splintering under the sheer weight of gigantic keys and landing on your foot. Or, if you put your keys in your pocket, vividly see your pocket being ripped apart from the sharp knife-like serrations of your keys, with shreds of material flying up and hitting you in the face.

Forgetting the whereabouts of keys is just one example of absent-mindedness. Many times people forget if they have locked the door to their house. To remember this, simply get a mental picture of your head sticking out of the door knob with a closed padlock piercing through your nose.

Other common examples of absent-mindedness are leaving your car lights on or forgetting where you put your eyeglasses. A mental picture that communicates your lights are off could be your hand breaking through your headlight—which means your lights aren't even working, much less on! One way to remember where you left your eyeglasses could be shown by the visual image of hundreds of glasses dancing across your desktop scattering your papers all around.

There are an endless number of mental flip books that can conjure up in your mind's eye to help you dramatically improve your ability of recall. Your key resources are imagination and emotion. Remember, if the picture is boring, jazz it up. Use action, exaggeration, and quantity. Always put yourself in the picture and observe with all your senses to get the clearest, most vivid picture possible. When you do, you will be engaging not only the intellectual memory of your mind but the emotional memory of your body.

The Link System is only the first of four systems you can use to boost your memory power. But, it is also a process that is used in all the systems yet to come. If you're ready, then move on to the second (and more powerful) memory system called the Loci System.

# The Loci System

Congratulations on progressing through the first *Photographic Mind Workshop* where you learned how to boost your ability to remember with the simple and effective Link System. Through this powerful process you mentally visualized two new pieces of dissimilar information in a crazy, illogical, bizarre manner, and then locked in that image with emotion.

The Link System requires a lot of imagination to keep the mental flip book going until you reach the end of the list of items. If you found that challenging, you'll probably find this next memory system is easier because it takes the unpredictable story order out of the picture—or rather it gives you a constant setting that is used over and over again. That setting will be your own Private Retreat. It's a setting you will become very familiar with through the exercises in the next two *Photographic Mind Workshops*.

This memory system is called the Loci System—"Loci" meaning place. It is Latin in origin and can be traced back to the time of the great Greek and Roman orators who used the Loci System to recite speeches with unfailing accuracy by associating each major point of the speech with a different room in their home.

There is an interesting legend that surrounds the beginnings of this system. Let's go back in time as we recreate the tragic occurrence that ironically enlightened the world to the memory power of the human mind.

## The Legend of the Loci System

The era is 500 B.C. and the setting is a very formal banquet in a beautiful structure reminiscent of early Greek architecture. Only the most powerful individuals of the city have been invited to attend this incredible show of opulence of fine food and drink.

The banquet has just begun, and the Greek poet Simonides is performing for this prestigious group of people, reciting his poetry with the greatest of passion, for this is indeed his performance of a lifetime. Having recited his poetry to the honored guests gathered around a huge banquet table, Simonides left the festivities and wandered outside the building reveling in his glory on this beautiful summer's day.

Suddenly he heard what sounded like a thunderclap shattering through the air, yet there wasn't a cloud in the sky. To his horror, he realized that the deafening sound was not a thunderclap at all, but the devastating collapse of the immense roof looming high above the guests seated at the banquet. Columns tumbled, stone was crushed into fine particles, and tragically not one of the honored guests survived. In fact, the bodies were so badly mangled by falling debris that none of them could be identified, and city officials feared they would never truly know who died on that fateful day.

*Yet Simonides approached the officials with the names of everyone seated at the banquet table.* When asked how he knew this information, (for there was no guest list to be had) Simonides replied that he simply visualized everyone sitting at the banquet table. By conjuring up a mental image of the banquet table and going from seat to seat he could remember all of the guests in attendance that day.

The theory here, and the basic underlying premise behind the success of this memory method, is that you can better remember people or objects if each is associated with a different location. This is today called the Loci System—again, "Loci" meaning place. And its ability to aid in the memory process has been widely known since this fateful day in Greece over 2,400 years ago.

## How the Loci System Works

Using the Loci System is as simple as imagining yourself walking through your house. Specifically, you take a mental tour of a house (or other building you are familiar with) by walking through four different rooms and noticing five different objects in each room. This gives you a total of 20 standard objects or props you can use like cue cards. Each prop is then linked to an item that you want to remember—whether it is an item on a grocery list, or an errand on a "To

Do" list, or even a point in a speech.

In other words, you are linking "prop one" with "item one" and "prop two" with "item two." Unlike the Link System, where you are forming a link between two new pictures, in the Loci System you are forming a link between a standard visual prop that you already know and a new item of information that you can visualize. In essence, the 20 props in the Loci System are permanent pictures you already have in your memory.

The Loci method works so well because it gives you a sequence for effectiveness (such as the sequence of the letters in the word HOMES to identify the 5 Great Lakes) without tying you too tightly to the logic (as in needing to find a word such as HOMES to fit the items you need to know).

## A Memory System for Your Left and Right Brain

The Loci is the best of both worlds and truly lets both sides of your brain support each other. It offers the logical left brain a linear model by supplying a predictable order of the 20 known props (as opposed to the free-wheeling unpredictable order of escalating events in the Link story). Along with this logic comes the comfort in knowing that this same order will be repeated over and over and over again.

And yet it leaves the visual right brain equally as happy, for while the Loci System does have a definite order, it still retains the free-flowing world of crazy, illogical, bizarre pictures that the playful right brain enjoys. The right brain, first of all, needs to get those 20 props into a visual format. Even better is the fact that your right brain will have the luxury of time to do this task. As this is a standard set of images you will call up again and again, you can afford to spend some time creating these mental pictures.

The Loci is also well-suited for your right brain because it still requires it to perform the split-second free-flowing crazy, illogical and bizarre imaging for the linking of the new incoming items with the 20 standard props.

In addition, the Loci System also makes good use of your emotional memory. For, as you will see in the upcoming *Photographic Mind Workshop*, the setting used for this exercise is an imaginary get-away home called your own Private Retreat. The interactive manner in which you come to learn its props will allow you to bond with each one with a tremendous amount of feeling.

---

## Three Ground Rules

Very shortly you will begin a guided tour through your Private Retreat via a set of architect's blueprints and designer's sketches. Along this tour we will identify 20 loci props for you to put into your memory. Before you go on this tour however, please become familiar with these three ground rules:

• **The first rule is to walk from room to room in a sequential order**. No backtracking is allowed. The order is very important to give a solid structure to this system.

• **The second rule is to scan each room in the same direction**. You are scanning each room in your Private Retreat for the five props it contains. The direction of our scan is counter clockwise.

• **The third ground rule is that there is no repetition of props**. Once we pick a table in the kitchen, we cannot pick a table in any other room. By having two of the same article in your 20 standard props you would not gain the full benefit of this system.

Again, the reason this system works is because it is based on 20 props (presented in a predictable order), all of which are both totally distinguishable from the other and at the same time very familiar to you.

---

As we take our mental caravan, let your right brain paint the images of the props with vivid detail and clarity and remember to engage all your senses. *Hear the music being played on the piano, smell the scent of pine logs burning in the fireplace, taste the exotic flavor of the coffee whose rich aroma is drifting through the air, see the hundreds of books that fill the bookcase built into the wall, and feel your body relax as you ease into the bubbling warmth of the hot springs.*

This is your Private Retreat. And it is the setting of one of the most powerful holistic memory tools you will ever come to know. Record these surroundings with all of your emotions by exploring through all your senses. The goal here is to engage your intellectual memory to visualize your props and to use your emotional memory to lock those images into memory.

## Photographic Mind Workshop: My Private Retreat

## Step 1: Active Learning Session

To enhance your experience of the material please play the *Accelerated Learning Music* soundtrack (located on Track #2 of your *Brain Supercharger* CD) while you complete the following workshop exercise.

During this step you will follow along with the architect's blueprints and designer's sketches as we take a mental caravan of your Private Retreat. Along the tour you will discover the 20 Loci Props that will be the basis of this powerful memory system.

Look at the pictures as you mentally read the words below each prop. As you do, let your right brain paint that image with detail and clarity. See the colors, see the shape, see the size. Engage all your senses. Feel the cloth of the fabric on the couch, hear the chime of the clock, smell the pine sent of the logs burning in the fireplace. Bring in your emotions by observing through all your senses. As this is a holistic approach to memory, be sure to use your intellectual memory to visualize your props and your emotional memory to seal in those images that you are vividly creating.

Later in this session you'll be asked to verbalize the props—out loud. The powerful sensory triad of seeing, reading, and verbalizing the material will have you memorizing at an accelerated rate.

### Room 1: The Living Room

*In room one, **the living room**, the first prop is the **grand piano**. It is welcoming you to your Private Retreat with your favorite song. Listen to it*

*play for you now and take a seat on the second prop, which is the **Queen Ann chair**.*

*As you sit down, feel the texture of the striping on the burgundy, green and beige fabric with your fingers as you ease yourself back into the feathery*

*cushion. Look around the room. To your right is the third prop, the **marble fireplace**. Breathe in the scent of pine logs whose embers are glowing brightly.*

*Directly in front of the fireplace is your fourth prop, a beautiful **Oriental rug**. Look closely. The intricate design is really a circular menagerie of emerald peacocks, yellow-eyed tigers and midnight blue pandas in a wreath of silken shoots of bamboo intertwining the species in an eternal dance.*

*The rug runs across the entire length of the floor, ending where it meets your*

*next prop, which is the **cherry wood desk**. Raise out of your chair now and walk over to the desk.*

*It is a drop-leaf secretary style, and the leaf is open, exposing the many cubicles. Peeking inside these cubicles you find them filled with your own personal memoirs—letters from an old lover, newspaper clippings about important events in your life, plus pictures of you from childhood birthday parties, prom nights and casual shots with friends you haven't seen in years.*

*As you browse through these items an aroma catches your attention. Follow it now.*

## Room 2: The Kitchen

*The aroma takes you into the second room, **the kitchen**, and draws you to the*

*first prop in this room, the **espresso machine**, which has brewed an exotic coffee for you.*

*The espresso machine is sitting on top of the second prop in this room, the*

***green tiled cooking island**, whose tiles are monogrammed with your initials. This cooking island runs the entire length of the kitchen and as you walk*

*around it you are lead directly to the third prop which is the **walk-in pantry**.*

*The door is open and you step inside. The shelves are lined with a red gingham paper and stocked with the many foods you enjoyed growing up as a child. Your favorite cereal is there, along with an opened package of the cookies you used to eat after school. Take one now.*

*In fact, pick up the whole package and come sit down at the next prop, which*

*is an **oak table**. It is a round table, with a massive center pedestal. Let the cookie crumbs fall to the table, then blow them away and let them fall to the floor.*

*Now, you need some milk to wash them down, so let's get up and walk to your*

*next prop, which of course is the **refrigerator**. It is unlike any refrigerator you* *have ever seen for it has mirrored doors, giving you a full length view of yourself. And look, you are naked! But then again, this is your Private Retreat, so why shouldn't you be?*

### Room 3: The Entertainment Room

*Suddenly you hear a gong. Oh no, is that the doorbell? You can't possibly answer it without being dressed! The chiming is continuing. But wait, it is not a door chime, but the chiming of a clock. This is your next prop. Follow the sound and you will find that it takes you into the third room of your private retreat, which is the **entertainment room**.*

*As you enter this high tech multi-media room you are met by the bellowing*

***grandfather clock** whose moon face dial is smiling serenely at you.*

*Adjacent to the clock is your next prop, a fully stocked **wet bar**. Looking past the bar your attention is immediately directed to your next prop, the **seven***

***foot television screen** at the far end of the room, which is playing some video footage of you.*

*Come on in and take a seat on your next prop, the **black leather couch.** The smooth leather seems to caress your bare skin. What a luxurious feeling. What a magnificent room. It's a theater. It's a concert hall. And it's a library too—just look at the hundreds of books lining your next prop—the **built-in***

***bookcase.***

*One book in particular seems to catch your attention. You walk over to it and as you pull it from the shelf, the entire bookcase begins to revolve. Suddenly you find yourself on the other side of the wall, in the fourth and final room in your Loci.*

## Room 4: The Tropical Sun Room

*To your amazement you are now in a **tropical sun room**. As you revolve into it, you are greeted by a warm moist air carrying the scents of lush foliage and the sounds of rushing water.*

*A **sea grass hammock**, your first prop in this room, hangs between two dwarfed palm trees whose broad leafed palms are rustling in the still air, as if someone had just brushed against them. Perhaps you are not alone here.*

*You glance quickly around, but all you see are your next two props—a*

***saltwater aquarium** filled with hungry sharks and a **gurgling river rock waterfall** lined with smoothed stone washed steps. You decide to climb up the steps.*

*As your foot glides from stone to stone you feel yourself being watched and look up expectantly, only to discover a pair of cockatoos staring at you from*

*the fourth prop, a **gilded bird cage**. They screech at you and you relax with a laugh, feeling secure now that you are indeed alone.*

*With a final step you crest the ledge of the waterfall where you discover your*

*last prop—and biggest surprise—a **bubbling hot springs**. And as you ease your body into it you suddenly realize that no, you are not alone.*

## Chunking the Prop Phrases

Visualizing your Private Retreat is similar to taking a relaxation exercise because of the sheer beauty of the surroundings. With such powerful imagery, the 20 props of this retreat are easy to learn and recall—especially because of the fact that the rank order of each prop is not important. For example, you do not need to know, that the fireplace is number three. *What you do need to know is what comes both before and after the fireplace.* In other words, you need to know the sequential order of the props.

Let's take a second mental caravan through your Private Retreat. Only this time, let's chunk the phrases describing each prop and increase your power of recall by verbalizing—out loud—each phrase.

As you say the names of the props, mentally see each one in vivid detail with all your senses, bringing in all your emotions. Hear the music playing on the piano and the ticking on the clock, see the intricate design in the oriental rug, smell the coffee brewing in the kitchen, taste the cookie you are eating, see your naked body in the mirrors of the refrigerator doors, and imagine your surprise when you pull that book out of the shelf causing the wall to revolve.

Relax and visualize the tropical sun room to be the beautiful island paradise of your dreams. This is your Private Retreat. Take your time. At this point, speed is not important. Your goal is to be able to create vivid mental images by engaging your intellectual memory and your emotional memory. Breathe in the moist heavy air as you mentally walk up those river smoothed stones of the waterfall. Smell the lush foliage all around you. And hear the screeching of the cockatoos above your head.

Then as you rise over the top ledge of the waterfall, relive your surprise as you discover the gurgling hot springs. And imagine who is there waiting for you. Let these emotions come into play. The more you do, the easier and faster you will be able to recall the 20 loci props of your Private Retreat.

Please recite (out loud) the following chunked word phrases. As you do, visualize with all your senses to bring the surroundings of your Private Retreat alive in your mind.

*In room one, the **living room**, the first prop is the **grand piano**.*

*The second prop is the **Queen Ann chair**.*

*The third prop is the **marble fireplace**.*

*The fourth prop is the **oriental rug**.*

*The fifth prop is the **cherry wood desk**.*

*In room two, **the kitchen**, the first prop is the **espresso machine**.*

*The second prop is the **green-tiled cooking island**.*

*The third prop is the **walk-in pantry**.*

*The fourth prop is the **oak table**.*

*The fifth prop is the mirrored **refrigerator**.*

*In room three, the **entertainment room**, the first prop is the **grandfather clock**.*

*The second prop is the **wet bar**.*

*The third prop is the **seven foot television screen**.*

*The fourth prop is the **black leather couch**.*

*The fifth prop is the **built-in bookcase**.*

*In room four, the **tropical sun room**, the first prop is the **sea grass hammock**.*

*The second prop is the **saltwater aquarium**.*

*The third prop is the **river rock waterfall**.*

*The fourth prop is the **gilded bird cage**.*

*and the fifth prop is the **bubbling hot springs**.*

Your Private Retreat offers you a wonderful escape to relax yourself and enjoy a quiet moment. And very soon you will tap into its real power, which is to help you remember 20 items quickly and easily. But first, you need to be able to reconnect with these props automatically. In Step 2 you will learn how and lock these props into your memory.

## Step 2: Passive Learning Session

The same 20 loci props of your Private Retreat you learned in the Active Learning Session are illustrated below without the use of any words. Spend the next two minutes gazing at them. As this session is designed for unconscious learning, allowing your mind to wander will give you the maximum benefit. Try not to concentrate on any one image that you see.

Feel yourself flow around the room from one prop to the next in a smooth sweeping motion. Let the left brain lead you in the proper sequential order while your right brain fills in the details of the prop. And let your senses add to the depth of the image by bringing in feelings, smells, and all the sights, sounds and tastes of the props. Just relax and let your mind open as you sweep through the whole scene.

**Room 1: The Living Room**

**Room 2: The Kitchen**

**Room 3: The Entertainment Room**

**Room 4: The Tropical Sun Room**

## Visual Clustering

By now, your Private Retreat should be intimately familiar to you in an emotional and visual context that draws on the strengths of both the logical left brain and the visual right brain as well as the emotional memory of your body. In the time it took you to scan the above illustrations you could have mentally reeled through each prop in your Private Retreat ten or more times. The reason for this is that your mind can think faster than you can talk, as you already experienced from the previous Link exercise where you mentally came to the end of your flip book before you finished reading the words.

Are you beginning to believe that you do indeed have a photographic mind that thinks more rapidly in pictures than you can write, type, or talk? Your belief in this idea will speed you along through this course. It's just amazing how fast you can whip through your Loci props after practicing them for a very short period of time. And the following tip will allow you to visualize your 20 Loci props even faster. It's a form of chunking, called visual clustering. Here's how it works.

Imagine that every room in your Loci System has a cathedral ceiling—a high vaulted ceiling that comes to a point at the top. Then, see yourself as a surveillance camera perched on the very highest point of that ceiling. From this viewpoint you could nearly simultaneously see every one of your props in the room at the same time. You could flash through them in less than a second. Try that right now in each of the four rooms by doing the following:

*In your mind's eye, give yourself the vantage point of a surveillance camera high in the ceiling so that in an instant you can cluster the five props together and see your groupings in a flash. As you do this, try not to mentally say the name of each prop—just let the image cluster in each room flash before your eyes.*

By doing this in each room you will be able to visualize your entire Loci System in a few mere seconds—still in vivid detail, full of emotional impact and as clearly as if those props were right in front of your eyes.

To help lock-in your lesson please play the *Super Memory Transformation* Soundtrack (located on Track #3 of your *Brain Supercharger* CD). Put the book aside for now and make sure to use stereo headphones. Find a comfortable position & quiet place where you can rest undisturbed for the next 30 minutes.

## Step 3: Assessment

Your final step in this workshop is to test your recall of the 20 props in the Loci System. They will form the background, or the standard set of mental images, that will be linked to the information you want to recall. The next workshop gives you the opportunity to try out this memory system, but before you can move on you need to demonstrate your ability to remember these 20 props with unfailing ease.

On the lines below please write the names of each room in your Private Retreat and the names of the props (in order) that appear in each room. Then compare your list to the answers provided and write your total number of correct answers on the score line (each correct answer is worth one point).

### Loci Prop List Recall

Room #1: _____

Prop: _____

Prop: _____

Prop: _____

Prop: _____

Prop: _____

Room #2: _____

Prop: _____

Prop: _____

Prop: _____

Prop: _____

Prop: _____


Room #3: _____

Prop: _____

Prop: _____

Prop: _____

Prop: _____

Prop: _____


Room #4: _____

Prop: _____

Prop: _____

Prop: _____

Prop: _____

Prop: _____


Your Total Score: _____


(Answers: *Room #1: The living room*—grand piano, Queen Ann chair, marble fireplace, oriental rug, cherry wood desk. *Room #2: The kitchen*—espresso machine, green-tiled cooking island, walk-in pantry, oak table, mirrored refrigerator. *Room #3: The entertainment room*—grandfather clock, wet bar, seven foot television screen, black leather couch, built-in bookcase. *Room #4: The tropical sun room*—sea grass hammock, saltwater aquarium, river rock waterfall, gilded bird cage, bubbling hot springs)


By now you should feel very comfortable with your Loci blueprint of your Private Retreat. You should be able to see it as 20 individual props. And you should also be able to see it as four clusters of five props each. If you remembered all of your props in perfect order, you are ready to read the remainder of this chapter. If, however, the props are not firmly implanted in your memory, (or you missed more than 2 answers) please review Steps 1 and 2 and retake the test before reading on.

## Creating a Blueprint of Your Own Home

Many people carry around in their heads a number of blueprints created with the Loci System. This enables them to recall 40, 60, 80, 100, or more bits of information with ease. After you have become proficient with using your Private Retreat Loci blueprint learned in this workshop, you can further develop your memory power with additional Loci blueprints based on houses that are familiar to you.

You learned the ground rules of creating a blueprint at the beginning of this workshop. They are repeated here for you:

- The first rule is to walk from room to room in a sequential order without backtracking.
- The second rule is to scan each room in the same direction.
- The third ground rule is to not repeat props.

Again, the reason this system works is because it is based on 20 props presented in a predictable order—all of which are both totally distinguishable from the other and at the same time very familiar to you.

Another helpful hint in picking out your props is to select items that are either large in size or elicit a strong emotion in you. A common thread that weaves throughout each memory system in this course is the involvement of both your intellectual and emotional memory. As you have already discovered from the Link System, attributes such as quantity and size aid in your ability to recall. Props that are enormous in size or massive in weight are simply easier to recall.

Yet, don't neglect a prop that is small in size but highly charged with emotion. For example, a souvenir cup and saucer in a curio cabinet that belonged to your mother, or an old and faded picture of your grandparents in a frame sitting on a coffee table, while small in size, can be very effective props. These props are simply unforgettable because they have ingrained a very deep memory trace. If you can, find props that combine the attribute of exaggeration (either large or small) with the added benefit of an emotional connection.

This is the beauty of the Loci System—it is ultimately familiar to you in an emotional and visual context which draws on the strengths of both the logical left brain and the visual right brain as well as the emotional memory of your body. This system works so well because it asks you to create links between new incoming information with the 20 standard props that you have already created in your memory. The upcoming *Photographic Mind Workshop* shows you step-by-step how to use this process in a challenging memory task.

## How to Use Your Loci Props as "Mental Pegs"

In the previous workshop you learned the second powerful memory system of this course—the Loci System—and you locked into memory the 20 loci props of your own Private Retreat. Now that you have your own personal Loci System firmly implanted in your memory, let's put it to use.

This system can first of all be used to remember items on a list, as with the Link System. And it has even greater value in its ability to help you recall stories, speeches, or points in a sales presentation. For your first experience with your own Loci System though, let's try the easier memory tasks of the two—remembering lists.

The way you use the Loci System for recalling lists is very similar to the Link System. You take two mental images and bring them together in a crazy, illogical, bizarre way, then seal in that image with emotion.

The difference between the two systems however, is that the Link System links "item one" to "item two" and "item two" to "item three" and so on, as with the eggs sledding on sizzling bacon, which is going down the mountain of frozen milk. In the Loci System, on the other hand, you are associating one new item with an image you already have stored in your mind—your first prop. *The props are not linked together.* Rather they exist as individual units and you simply know which prop comes next.

As you do this, think of yourself as "hanging" the grocery list item on each prop. This prop is in effect, acting as a "mental peg" on which to hang that information, much as a peg on a wall rack acts as a physical peg on which you hang your coat. When you want to recall your grocery list you simply go over to your mental peg rack of Loci props and pull each item off its prop.

All the techniques you used to visualize your mental images with the Link System apply equally as well to the Loci System. Use action, exaggeration, and quantity to engage your intellectual memory. Involve all your senses to bring in your emotional memory as well. And put yourself in the picture. Your goal is to create vivid mental pictures, full of clarity and descriptive detail.

The following workshop gives you the opportunity to hang a list of 20 grocery items (different from the previous list) on your 20 Loci props from your Private Retreat. After you have been taken through this process step-by-step you will be ready to use the Loci system to commit any list to memory.

## Photographic Mind Workshop: Shopping the Loci Way

### Step 1: Active Learning Session

To enhance your experience of the material please play the *Accelerated Learning Music* soundtrack (located on Track #2 of your *Brain Supercharger* CD) while you complete the following workshop exercise.

During this step you will follow along in your book as you see how the 20 grocery items are pegged, or hung, onto the 20 loci props of your Private Retreat.

Look at the images as you silently read the words below each prop that describe how the prop and grocery item have been linked together. Remember to engage your right brain to fill in the color and details of the image to bring it vividly alive in your mind. Use all your senses to experience this process of hanging the items onto your props.

Hear the blocks of cheese playing the piano. See the pickle throwing the Queen Ann chair out the window. Feel the butter melting all over your fingers as you use it to light the fire in the marble fireplace. Smell the ham cooking in the bubbling hot springs all around you as you go bobbing for your dinner! Simply let your emotions run wild to lock all these images into your memory.

Later in this session you'll recite the phrases that describe how each of the 20 items are hung onto your Loci props. The powerful sensory triad of seeing, reading, and verbalizing the material will have you memorizing at an accelerated rate.

The first five items on this list are *cheese, pickles, butter, tomatoes,* and *lettuce.* Your first five Loci props in your first room, the living room are *grand piano, Queen Anne chair, marble fireplace, oriental rug,* and *cherry wood desk.* Visually hanging each item on the corresponding prop you see:

*Dozens of blocks of **cheese** playing the keys on the grand piano.*

*A huge **pickle** picking up the Queen Anne chair and throwing it out the window.*

*See yourself building a fire in the marble fireplace with sticks of **butter** instead of sticks of wood, and feel the butter melting all over your hand.*

*See hundreds of **tomatoes** being thrown at the oriental rug, their juices staining the fabric.*

*See and hear the drawers of the cherry wood desk flying open and spitting out*

*heads of **lettuce**.*

Do you get the picture here? You use intellectual memory full of descriptive detail such as colors, size, quantity, plus emotional detail charged with feelings— be it either a positive emotion, such as love or laughter, or a negative one such as disgust or fear. Remember to see all of the action, and put yourself into the picture as much as possible.

The next five items on this list are *muffins, yogurt, pop, coffee* and *toothpaste*. Your five Loci props in your second room, the kitchen, are *espresso machine, green-tiled cooking island, walk-in pantry, oak table*, and *mirrored refrigerator*. Visually hanging each item on the corresponding prop you see:

*Teeny tiny **muffins** "brewing" through the spigot of the espresso machine instead of coffee.*

*A giant container of **yogurt** spilling all over the tiles of the cooking island, covering up your initials.*

*See and hear bottles of **pop** exploding in your face as you walk into the pantry.*

*See grains of **coffee** erupting right up through the pedestal of the oak table like a volcano spewing lava.*

*See **toothpaste** smeared all over the refrigerator, blocking out your image in its mirrored doors.*

The next five items on this list are *grapes, tuna fish, peanuts, frozen juice*, and *paper towels*. Your next five Loci props in your third room, the entertainment room are *grandfather clock, wet bar, seven foot television screen, black leather couch*, and *built-in bookcase*. Visually hanging each item on the corresponding prop you see:

*The hands on the grandfather clock stuffing bunches of **grapes** into the moonfaced dial who is spitting the seeds at you.*

*Tuna fish jumping from one cocktail glass to the next on the wet bar.*

*See yourself hurling bags of **peanuts** at the seven foot television screen, shattering the screen into a million pieces.*

*Feel yourself sitting naked among hundreds of cans of **frozen juice** strewn all*

*over the black leather couch.*

*See columns of **paper towels** filling the built-in bookcase instead of books.*

The last five items on this list are *sugar, flour, cucumbers, aluminum foil*, and *ham*. Your last five Loci props in your last room, the tropical sun room are *sea grass hammock, saltwater aquarium, river rock waterfall, gilded bird cage, bubbling hot springs*. Visually hanging each item on the corresponding prop you see:

*A giant bag of **sugar** emptying its contents into the sea grass hammock and you are in the hammock being buried under the mountains of sugar.*

*Bags of **flour** shackled to the tails of the sharks weighing them down to the*

*bottom of the saltwater aquarium, just as a ball and chain are shackled to prisoners.*

*Feel and see enormous* **cucumbers** *come tumbling down the river rock waterfall knocking you down to the bottom.*

*See many tiny rolls of* **aluminum foil** *decorating the gilded bird cage with their shiny material like tinsel all over a Christmas tree.*

*See and smell Frisbee size slices of* **ham** *cooking in the bubbling hot springs all around you as you go bobbing for your dinner!*

Was that easy for you to see these images? If not, be patient—the more you work with this process, the easier it will be for you to vividly imagine these crazy, illogical, bizarre pictures. You can make it easy for yourself by using the guidelines you learned earlier—lots of action, exaggeration, quantity, putting yourself in the picture and using all your senses.

## Chunking the Prop Phrases

Let's go through the 20 props a second time. This time, you'll isolate each individual prop and chunk the phrase describing the way the item is hung on the prop. Plus you'll increase your power of recall by verbalizing—out loud—each phrase.

As you say the phrases, remember to feel the action. Engage your intellectual memory through the devices of exaggeration and quantity. Remember to put yourself in the action whenever possible. Your goal is to really experience this scene by using all of your senses. This is your Private Retreat. All of these props are your possessions. Let your emotions—anger, sadness, fear, humor—come into play as you see these 20 grocery items running wild through your dream house.

Please recite (<u>out loud</u>) the following chunked Loci prop phrases.

*Dozens of blocks of **cheese** playing the keys on the grand piano.*

*A huge **pickle** picking up the Queen Anne chair and throwing it out the window.*

*Building a fire in the marble fireplace with sticks of **butter**, and feeling the butter melting all over my hand.*

*Hundreds of **tomatoes** being thrown at the oriental rug, their juices staining the fabric.*

*The drawers of the cherry wood desk flying open and spitting out heads of **lettuce**.*

*Teeny tiny **muffins** "brewing" through the spigot of the espresso machine.*

*A giant container of **yogurt** spilling all over the tiles of the cooking island, covering up my initials.*

*Bottles of **pop** exploding in my face as I walk into the pantry.*

*Grains of **coffee** erupting right up through the pedestal of the oak table like a volcano spewing lava.*

***Toothpaste** smeared all over the refrigerator, blocking my image in its mirrored doors.*

*The hands on the grandfather clock stuffing bunches of **grapes** into the moonfaced dial who is spitting the seeds at me.*

***Tuna fish** jumping from one cocktail glass to the next on the wet bar.*

*I am hurling bags of **peanuts** at the seven foot television screen, shattering the screen into a million pieces.*

*I am sitting naked among hundreds of cans of **frozen juice** strewn all over the black leather couch.*

*Columns of **paper towels** filling the built-in bookcase instead of books.*

*A giant bag of **sugar** pouring all over me, burying me as I relax in the sea grass hammock.*

*Bags of **flour** shackled to the tails of the sharks weighing them down to the bottom of the saltwater aquarium.*

*Enormous **cucumbers** tumbling over the river rock waterfall knocking me down to the bottom.*

*Many tiny rolls of **aluminum foil** decorating the gilded bird cage like tinsel all over a Christmas tree.*

*Frisbee size slices of **ham** cooking in the bubbling hot springs all around me as I bob for my dinner!*

Did those crazy, illogical, bizarre images become clearer to you this time? Could you visualize them in greater detail and at a faster pace?

> *What are you using to build a fire?*
> *What happens when you walk into the pantry?*
> *What surrounds you as you sit on the black leather couch?*
> *And finally, what is happening to you as you climb the river rock waterfall?*

This is the fun way to lock things into your memory. And it is easy for you to do because you are using holistic memory—using the intellectual memory of your brain to conjure up these crazy, illogical, bizarre images and using the emotional memory of your body to lock those pictures into memory.

## Step 2: Passive Learning Session

In the previous lesson you learned about visual clustering, where you imagined yourself to be a surveillance camera at the top of a high point in each room. At this vantage point you could mentally flash on all the props nearly instantaneously.

The following scene gives you an example of visual clustering with the grocery items hung on the Loci props. Spend the next two minutes gazing at each room of props. Every so often close your eyes and try to flash on a room. As this session is designed for unconscious learning, allowing your mind to wander will give you the maximum benefit. Try not to concentrate on any one element that you see.

Feel yourself sweep the room in a quick click of the camera's eye. Your left brain is leading you in the proper sequential order while your right brain feels all the action going on with input from your senses. Just relax and let your mind open as you take everything in. At the end of the two minutes, do a final mental flash of the entire four rooms. You will find that as you call up each prop you automatically see the item popping into your head.

**The Entertainment Room**

## The Kitchen

## The Living Room

## The Tropical Sun Room

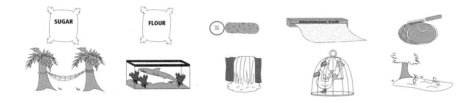

To help lock-in your lesson please play the *Super Memory Transformation* Soundtrack (located on Track #3 of your *Brain Supercharger* CD). Put the book aside for now and make sure to use stereo headphones. Find a comfortable position & quiet place where you can rest undisturbed for the next 30 minutes.

## Step 3: Assessment

At the end of Step 2 you were probably flashing on the entire grocery list in seconds. Now however, you need to slow yourself down to write the items on the lines below in order of their appearance in your Loci blueprint. (Write the grocery items only, not the Loci props.) When you are done, compare your list to the answers provided and write your total number of correct answers on the score line (each correct answer is worth one point).

### Loci Grocery List Recall

1. _____

2. _____

3. _____

4. _____

5. _____

6. _____

7. _____

8. _____

9. _____

10. _____

11. _____

12. _____

13. _____

14. _____

15. _____

16. _____

17. _____

18. _____

19. _____

20. _____

Your Total Score: _____

*(Answers: cheese, pickles, butter, tomatoes, lettuce, muffins, yogurt, pop, coffee, toothpaste, grapes, tuna fish, peanuts, frozen juice, paper towels, sugar, flour, cucumbers, aluminum foil, ham)*

Now total your points. To continue on with this course, you need to have recalled all 20 grocery list items in their correct order. If you didn't get a perfect score, ask yourself these two questions:

- *Do I know the props?* If not, practice recalling just your props.
- *Can I see the grocery item hanging on the prop?*

If not, try hanging it on your prop in a different way. Involve a different sense. For example, if you can't remember the toothpaste smeared all over the refrigerator, try another approach. See a smile on the refrigerator and then imagine it sticking out its tongue at you—but see the tongue as being a tube of toothpaste.

Remember to bring in your emotions through your senses. Make these pictures crystal clear in your mind. When you do, every grocery item will simply pop into your memory as quickly and easily as the props do. *The mind sees in pictures. The mind does not forget what it creates.* This system works so beautifully because it is a natural extension of how your mind and body remembers.

## Your On-Line Memory Scratch Pad

Every memory system in this course will save you time as it improves your memory. Each one allows you to make up lists of things without ever needing a pencil and paper. It's as if you have your own internal on-line memory scratch pad waiting for you to use wherever you are—whether you're stuck in traffic, riding up an elevator, standing in line or waiting for your computer to download a file. And even better, you will never lose this scratch pad (or the information that's on it) because it is stored in your memory.

The Loci blueprint of your Private Retreat holds 20 items. If you need to remember more items, you can create another Loci blueprint based on a floor in your home, your office building, or even the stores in a shopping mall. The only requirements are that the place is familiar to you and that the rooms present a sequential order to the props.

The Romans and Greeks were continually adding new Locis to their memory by familiarizing themselves with different buildings in their city. This system is infinitely expandable. And almost infinitely applicable to all your memory tasks.

The one disadvantage to the Loci System is that is does not allow you to directly access an item by knowing its position. For example, from the previous exercise, you don't know the name of the seventh item on the grocery list. You can get to it by mentally running through the first six items, but you can't freely recall the item based on its rank order. And while this is not important for lists, speeches or presentations, it is important if you are trying to recall the eighth president of the United States or the 10th of the original 13 colonies.

Many work-related memory tasks do involve directly assessing a specific ranked item. And while neither the Link nor the Loci System are effective for retrieving this information there is a system that can connect you to this information quickly and easily. It's called the Peg System. And you'll learn about it in the next chapter.

# The Peg System

**B**efore you read any further, take the time to congratulate yourself on how much you have improved your memory since the first few pages of this book. You now have learned two of the three powerful mnemonic processes—the Link and the Loci. And let's begin this chapter by asking a few questions to test your memory.

> *What were the eggs sledding on?*
> *What did the lemon chair lift fall into?*
> *What was squashing out of the diapers on the chicken?*
> *What was piloting the potato chip airplane through the*
>   *puffy clouds of rice?*

It all comes back to you, doesn't it? Why? <u>Because your mind thinks in pictures</u>—*it can create vivid mental images with action, exaggeration, by changing the quantity, putting you in the picture and using your emotions to lock in those images.* This is the emotional memory of your body working in harmony with the intellectual memory of your brain.

Now, let's test your memory on the Loci props of your Private Retreat.

> *What are your first five?*
> *Now the last five?*
> *Now run through the first five grocery list items from your Loci list.*

It's still there, isn't it? <u>These are powerful memory systems</u>. *And they work because they are a natural expansion of how your mind and body records memory—through categorizing, mapping the categories, and networking the information back and forth with neurotransmitters communicating from your senses, your body, and to your brain.*

There are holograms of memory traces throughout your body connecting you to all this information. As you read in Part I, you have a multi-dimensional architecture of memory available to you. The memory processes you learned in the previous *Photographic Mind Workshops* are allowing you to tap into the command system of access routes that let you retrieve the information quickly and easily. This next system, the Peg System, will expand your memory power infinitely more.

## How the Peg System Works

Similar to the Loci System, the Peg System uses "mental pegs" as a place to hang a piece of information. While the pegs in the Loci System were the 20 props in your Private Retreat, the pegs in this upcoming system are 20 items you find from your childhood in an old and abandoned garage.

Just as with the Loci props, these 20 items will become permanent parts of your memory, called mental pegs. You hang new information on each by visually imagining both the peg and the new information, then linking the two in a crazy, illogical, bizarre manner and locking in that mental image with emotion.

## Choosing Objects with Built-In Number Associations

Again, similar to the loci props, the mental pegs in this system are items that are easily pictured. But even better, each one has a natural association with a number 1 through 20. *The benefit here is that this allows you to intuitively know the rank order or position of the item you are remembering.*

For instance, item number 13 in the loci grocery list (that you memorized in the last *Photographic Mind Workshop*) was peanuts. Now, you wouldn't know that unless you mentally took a caravan through your first room, through your second room, and into your third room to your third prop. With the Peg System, you would know automatically that the 13th item was peanuts. Why? Because you would have a crystal clear image of a gigantic Planter's Peanut falling off a ladder. "A ladder," you may wonder—"why a ladder?" The reason is because the mental peg (or picture word) for number 13 in the Peg System is LADDER.

Think about that. *Why would the mental peg word for the number 13 be a ladder?* What is the association between 13 and ladder? What happens when you walk under a ladder? It brings you bad luck. What is an unlucky number?—13. You know it is unlucky to walk under a ladder. You know the number 13 is unlucky. *And therefore you know that the 13th peg in this system is a ladder.*

Every mental peg in this system is used in its rank order or numbered position because of its pre-existing association with that specific number. Just as the Loci System builds on the knowledge of the order of props in your Private Retreat that were locked into your memory, the Peg System also builds on the knowledge you already have—the numbers 1 through 20 and the association that connects these numbers to their mental peg word, as with 13 and ladder.

The upcoming *Photographic Mind Workshop* teaches you the remaining 19 picture words in the Peg System along with the association that makes it easy for you to connect each one to its peg number. But first, let's take a virtual journey through the setting of this workshop. Here you find an old abandoned garage, full of items from your childhood.

## A Garage Full of Memories

You're about to journey into a very old garage. The dilapidated structure sits at the far end of the yard of an old house, which is now boarded up and vacated. Within the hour both the house and the garage will be demolished to make way for your new office building. But now, all is quiet on this hot August day.

Standing in the cool shade of the back porch you see the garage. You walk down the porch steps to a stone gravel path overgrown with weeds. The path winds through what once must have been a garden. You follow it to a side door of the garage. The door is slightly ajar and it creaks heavily as you open it. The sun streams into the darkened garage in a shaft of light full of dancing dust particles.

You step into the doorway. The heavy musty smell reminds you of the hot, dry air in the attic on a summer's day. You look around. You see many things that remind you of your past. Next to the door is an old wooden step ladder. It is opened, and hanging from its supports is a metal compass on a brown and black lanyard. Underneath the ladder is a red tricycle. From the layers of dust on it you can tell it hasn't been ridden for a long time. Next to it lies a pair of old fashioned shoes with buckles. And you think of the nursery rhyme...*One, two, buckle my shoe.* In your mind you hear the laugher of children and wonder where the child is that once rode this tricycle, wore these shoes, and climbed on the ladder with compass in hand just like an explorer would race to the top of a hill to look out over the horizon.

As your eyes become accustomed to the darkness you look around. Leaning against the side of the garage is an old leather golf bag with various golf clubs. Next to it stands a pair of old wooden skis. At the bottom of the skis, on the dirt floor, is a toy holster and a six-shooter cap gun with a fake swivel barrel. You pick it up. A roll of red caps is still in it. You pull the trigger and a sharp clap ignites the dot of powder. As the puff of smoke escapes you hold the gun barrel up to your nose to inhale that familiar smell from your childhood.

You put the gun back down and notice a sheriff's badge covered in dust. You pick it up and blow away the dust to reveal a shiny gold star. You remember you had one just like it. But you haven't seen it in years. You go to put it down, but on second thought, you put it in your pocket—all this is going to be demolished soon anyway.

Suddenly you hear movement in the far end of the garage. Before you have the chance to react, a cat darts past you through the open door into the daylight. It must have been watching you from what appears to be a workbench in the far end of the garage. You walk over to the workbench.

Hanging over the workbench is a calendar. The month is February. There's a heart drawn around the 14th for Valentine's Day. The picture on the calendar is a Norman Rockwell painting of an old fashioned girl with her head in her hands with her lips puckered and a woeful expression on her face. The caption reads "Sweet 16 and Never Been Kissed."

Sitting in the middle of the workbench is an old fashioned cuckoo clock—a broken one, with it's various parts strewn out across the workbench. Both hands point to the twelve o'clock hour. A cracked fish aquarium sits at the far right of the workbench—inhabited only by a plastic octopus with eight outstretched tentacles. One of the tentacles is wrapped around a pirate holding a bottle of rum. This image triggers the lyrics from a song you heard long ago on the Pirates of the Caribbean ride in Disneyland: "Yo-ho-ho...a pirate's life for me. Fifteen men on a Dead Man's Chest. Yo-ho-ho...and a bottle of rum...a pirate's life for me."

Part of the glass from the fish tank is laying on the cover of a magazine. You look closer and see that the magazine is a very old and yellowed issue of Seventeen. The picture has been faded beyond recognition from the sunlight coming through the window above it.

On the window sill you notice the cap of a wide-mouthed jar. It holds a dime, a penny and a book of matches. You pick up the book of matches. It reads "The Seven-Heaven Truck Stop." You laugh at the cartooned image it shows of an 18-wheeler plowing through clouds as it passes through the proverbial pearly gates. Suddenly you stop laughing as you actually hear what sounds like an 18-wheeler coming right at you. In your horror you realize that sound is a bulldozer demolishing the garage.

Within seconds an ear-shattering crack slices through the silence as the bulldozer rips through the side of the garage opposite you. You run for the daylight of the open door and the roof heaves heavily before its final collapse. You dive into the daylight and land on the weeded path. Just seconds after you land, the door frame falls heavily around you, but luckily the door had already ripped free. There you lay motionless; your outstretched pose from your hands to your feet outlined by the jagged door frame, the "Seven-Heaven Truck Stop" matchbook still held in your hand.

## Photographic Mind Workshop: My Virtual Peg Board

### Step 1: Active Learning Session

To enhance your experience of the material please play the *Accelerated Learning Music* soundtrack (located on Track #2 of your *Brain Supercharger* CD) while you complete the following workshop exercise.

The story you just read held the 20 pegs (or picture-words for the numbers 1 through 20) for your Peg System. This peg list is illustrated on the next page. Please scan the list and try to determine the 20 pegs from the story and their associated number. Write the number and it's association next to each item in the list for each of the pegs. The way to do this is to ask yourself "What is the association between any of these pictures and a number 1 through 20?" You were given one of the pegs earlier—the ladder with number 13—with the association being "unlucky." You'll see it written in the list on the following page. Your challenge is to determine the other 19 pegs found in the story.

By asking your mind to discover the answer (rather than reading a list of the pegs and their association) you are inviting your brain to be a co-creator of this memory system. The importance of this, as you learned earlier, is that the brain simply does not forget what it creates.

Spend the next few minutes trying to fill out each peg on the following page. If you get stuck, try rereading the story. When you have filled in as many answers as you can, read the paragraphs that follow to see how many of your answers match. A completed Peg List follows this description for easy reference.

A little further into the workshop you'll be asked to verbalize out loud these pegs and their association with each number. The powerful sensory triad of seeing, reading, and verbalizing the material will have you memorizing at an accelerated rate.

| Peg Word | Number | Association |
|---|---|---|
| star | | |
| octopus | | |
| penny | | |
| dime | | |
| trycycle | | |
| cat | | |
| compass | | |
| shoes | | |
| heaven | | |
| ladder | 13 | unlucky |
| six-shooter | | |
| skis | | |
| magazine | | |
| heart | | |
| pirate | | |

| | |
|---|---|
| | fingers & toes |
| | clock |
| | 18-wheeler |
| | golf club |
| | lips |

### • Pegs for the numbers 1 through 5

*PENNY is the mental peg for the number 1.*

Now ask yourself, "What is the association between PENNY and 1?" This one is very obvious! The association that links number 1 with the mental peg PENNY is one cent. In the story, a penny was sitting in the jar cap on the window sill.

*SHOES is the mental peg for the number 2.*

Now ask yourself, "What is the association between SHOES and 2?" Don't think too hard—you'll go right past it. Here's a hint from the story: "One, two, buckle my _____." The association that links number 2 with the mental peg SHOES is a pair of shoes, which were on the floor of the garage.

*TRICYCLE is the mental peg for the number 3.*

Now ask yourself, "What is the association between TRICYCLE and 3?" The association that links number 3 with the mental peg TRICYCLE is three wheels. And I'm sure you remember the red tricycle from the story.

*COMPASS is the mental peg for the number 4.*

Now ask yourself, "What is the association between COMPASS and 4?" There's North, South, East, West...the \_\_\_\_ corners of the world. The association that links number 4 with the mental peg COMPASS is four directions. Do you remember where the compass was in the story? It was hanging from the ladder.

*STAR is the mental peg for number 5.*

Now ask yourself, "What is the association between STAR and 5?" You may need to think about this for a few seconds. Can you feel your mind searching, searching for the connection between STAR and the number 5? Remember the sheriff's star badge from the story? Mentally hold that star in your hand. How many points do you see? The association that links number 5 with the mental peg STAR is having five points.

### • Pegs for the Numbers 6 Through 10

*6-SHOOTER is the mental peg for number 6.*

Now ask yourself, "What is the association between a six-shooter and 6?" The association that links number 6 with the mental peg six-shooter is of course, the six barrels in the toy gun you found on the floor of the garage.

*HEAVEN is the mental peg for the number 7.*

Now ask yourself, "What is the association between HEAVEN and 7?" Unlike the other mental peg words, HEAVEN is more of an abstract word, than a concrete word.

In Part I you learned that concrete words are tangible items which are easy for you to picture. Abstract words are ones like NOURISHMENT, DULL, MATURE, that are hard to picture. Because you haven't actually seen HEAVEN you don't really know what it looks like. But when you hear the word HEAVEN, a picture definitely pops into your mind. People commonly see angels with halos on their heads and puffy white clouds all around, or St. Peter standing at the proverbial pearly gates.

In the story, the illustration on the matchbook cover picked up some of these images. Through them you can call on your intellectual memory to create a symbol for the word HEAVEN, since you don't have a real-life picture for that mental peg. This is known as symbolizing. In the association that links number 7 with the mental peg HEAVEN, your are using the well known expression of "7th heaven" as a symbol for the concept of heaven as a place of eternal bliss.

---

### The Power of Symbols

Symbolizing is a very useful technique in memory because there are many things you need to remember that are not concrete items. In other words, the word itself can't be visualized but it can be substituted by a symbol that is easy to picture.

Symbolism is a form of word substitution. It uses the metaphor making capacity of your right brain to translate an idea into an instantly recognizable picture. For instance, take the word LIBERTY. It's not a tangible thing—you can't hold it or touch it, and you can't hold up a picture of it. But you can symbolize it—meaning you can identify a picture that readily reminds you of the word LIBERTY.

One symbol could be the STATUE OF LIBERTY. You can see that. And you can easily associate it with LIBERTY. Using the Stature of Liberty as a symbol allows you to turn the intangible word LIBERTY into a tangible object filled with meaning and emotion.

---

*OCTOPUS is the mental peg for the number 8.*

Now ask yourself, "What is the association between OCTOPUS and 8?" The association that links number 8 with the mental peg OCTOPUS is 8 arms. And as you recall, there was an octopus in the aquarium on the workbench.

*CAT is the mental peg for the number 9.*

Now ask yourself, "What is the association between CAT and 9?" The association that links number 9 with the mental peg CAT is 9 lives. In the story, a cat darted past you as you stood in the doorway of the garage.

*DIME is the mental peg for the number 10.*

Now ask yourself, "What is the association between DIME and 10?" The association that links number 10 with the mental peg DIME is of course, 10 cents. In the story, a dime was sitting in the jar cap on the window sill.

### • Pegs for the Numbers 11 Through 15

*SKIS is the mental peg for the number 11.*

Now ask yourself, "What is the association between SKIS and 11?" The association that links number 11 with the mental peg SKIS is that image of the pair of skis in the story as they leaned against the garage wall side-by-side.

*CLOCK is the mental peg for the number 12.*

Now ask yourself, "What is the association between CLOCK and 12?" The association that links number 12 with the mental peg CLOCK is the cuckoo clock on the workbench having both hands pointing at the number 12.

*LADDER is the mental peg for the number 13.*

The association, as you already know, that links number 13 with the mental peg LADDER is unlucky. This was the first picture word you came across in the story.

*HEART is the mental peg for the number 14.*

Now ask yourself, "What is the association between HEART and 14?" The association that links number 14 with the mental peg HEART is February 14th or Valentine's Day, which in the story, had a heart drawn around this date on the calendar.

*PIRATE is the mental peg for the number 15.*

Now ask yourself, "What is the association between PIRATE and 15?" The association that links number 15 with the mental peg PIRATE, is the verse "Fifteen men on a Dead Man's Chest. Yo-ho-ho...and a bottle of rum...a pirate's life for me." symbolized by the pirate, which was held by the octopus in the story.

**• Pegs for the Numbers 16 Through 20**

*LIPS is the mental peg for the number 16.*

Now ask yourself, "What is the association between LIPS and 16?" The association that links number 16 with the mental peg LIPS is "Sweet 16 and never been kissed," which was the caption on the calendar picture.

*MAGAZINE is the mental peg for number 17.*

Now ask yourself, "What is the association between MAGAZINE and 17?" The association that links number 17 with the mental peg MAGAZINE is the popular SEVENTEEN MAGAZINE, on which the cracked piece of aquarium glass was found in the story.

*18-WHEELER is the mental peg for the number 18.*

Now ask yourself, "What is the association between 18-WHEELER and 18?" The association that links number 18 with the mental peg 18-WHEELER is, of course, number of wheels. In the story the bulldozer sounded like an 18-wheeler coming at you.

*GOLF CLUB is the mental peg for the number 19.*

Now ask yourself, "What is the association between GOLF CLUB and 19?" The association that links number 19 with the mental peg GOLF CLUB is the popular 19th hole of golf, which is the bar. As you recall, you saw a set of golf clubs in the garage.

*FINGERS & TOES is the mental peg for the number 20.*

Now ask yourself, "What is the association between FINGERS & TOES and 20?" The association that links number 20 with the mental peg FINGERS & TOES is your total number of fingers and toes. In the story the door frame narrowly missed your fingers and toes as it fell around you.

| Peg Word | Number | Association |
| --- | --- | --- |
| PENNY | 1 | A cent |
| SHOES | 2 | A pair or "one, two, buckle my shoe" |
| TRICYCLE | 3 | Having 3 wheels |
| COMPASS | 4 | Having 4 directions |
| STAR | 5 | Number of points |
| 6-SHOOTER | 6 | Number of barrels in the gun |
| HEAVEN | 7 | 7th heaven, place of eternal bliss |
| OCTOPUS | 8 | Number of arms |

| | | |
|---|---|---|
| CAT | 9 | Number of lives |
| DIME | 10 | Number of cents |
| SKIS | 11 | Together, side-by-side |
| CLOCK | 12 | Numbers on a face |
| LADDER | 13 | Unlucky |
| HEART | 14 | February 14, Valentine's Day |
| PIRATE | 15 | "Fifteen men on a dead man's chest... a pirate's life for me." |
| LIPS | 16 | Sweet sixteen and never been kissed |
| MAGAZINE | 17 | Seventeen Magazine |
| 18-WHEELER | 18 | Number of wheels |
| GOLF CLUB | 19 | The 19th hole of golf |
| FINGERS & TOES | 20 | Number of these that you have |

## Chunking the Peg List

Now that you understand the connection between the number and its mental peg, let's chunk the phrases describing each peg and its association to the specific number and verbalize this information—out loud—to increase your recall of these pegs.

As you say each phrase, mentally connect each picture-word to a number by its association, as if you were hanging each picture-word onto a hook in a gigantic Virtual Peg Board. Take your time. At this point, speed is not important. The goal is to be able to see the logic of each picture word through the association that connects the two. The better you are able to focus on this, the easier and faster you will be able to recall the 20 mental pegs.

Please recite (out loud) the following chunked word phrases. As you do, vividly see that mental peg, pictured crystal clear in your mind's eye. See it. Feel it. Touch it. Hold it. Smell it. Hear it. Let your emotions come in to seal in that memory.

PENNY is the mental peg for the number 1.

SHOES is the mental peg for the number 2.

TRICYCLE is the mental peg for the number 3.

COMPASS is the mental peg for the number 4.

STAR is the mental peg for number 5.

6-PACK is the mental peg for number 6.

HEAVEN is the mental peg for the number 7.

OCTOPUS is the mental peg for the number 8.

CAT is the mental peg for the number 9.

DIME is the mental peg for the number 10.

SKIS is the mental peg for the number 11.

CLOCK is the mental peg for the number 12.

LADDER is the mental peg for the number 13.

HEART is the mental peg for the number 14.

PIRATE is the mental peg for number 15.

LIPS is the mental peg for the number 16.

MAGAZINE is the mental peg for number 17.

18-WHEELER is the mental peg for the number 18.

GOLF CLUB is the mental peg for the number 19.

FINGERS & TOES is the mental peg for the number 20.

## Step 2: Passive Learning Session

The 20 pegs of your Virtual Peg Board that you learned in the Active Learning Session are illustrated below without the use of any words. Spend the next two minutes gazing at them. As this session is designed for unconscious learning, allowing your mind to wander will give you the maximum benefit. Try not to concentrate on any one item that you see.

Recall the story as you gaze around the garage. As your eyes see the picture associated with a mental peg, feel yourself mentally move that image onto the correct numbered position of the Virtual Peg Board you hold in your mind. It is not necessary to do these in any order for your mind intuitively knows the order based on the association in your memory. Just relax and let your mind open as you sweep through the whole scene and recall the story.

To help lock-in your lesson please play the *Super Memory Transformation* Soundtrack (located on Track #3 of your *Brain Supercharger* CD). Put the book aside for now and make sure to use stereo headphones. Find a comfortable position & quiet place where you can rest undisturbed for the next 30 minutes.

# Step 3: Assessment

You are now ready to test your recall of the 20 pegs in the Peg System. They will become your Virtual Peg Board, which like the Loci Props, form a standard set of mental images that will be linked to the information you want to recall. The next workshop gives you the opportunity to try out this memory system, but before you can move on, you need to demonstrate your ability to remember these 20 props easily and accurately.

Please write the mental pegs, or picture words, for each number below. You will notice that these are out of order. Again, the benefit of the Peg System is that it allows you to connect with any item of information instantly based on its rank order, or numbered position. Unlike the Link or Loci, it is not necessary to flip through a sequence of images to arrive at your desired answer.

After you are done, compare your list to the answers provided and write your total number of correct answers on the score line (each correct answer is worth one point).

### Peg List Recall

1. The mental peg for number 10 is _____

2. The mental peg for number 13 is _____

3. The mental peg for number 5 is _____

4. The mental peg for number 8 is _____

5. The mental peg for number 17 is _____

6. The mental peg for number 12 is _____

7. The mental peg for number 3 is _____

8. The mental peg for number 15 is _____

9. The mental peg for number 20 is _____

10. The mental peg for number 7 is _____

11. The mental peg for number 16 is _____

12. The mental peg for number 19 is _____

13.  The mental peg for number 2 is _____

14. The mental peg for number 6 is _____

15. The mental peg for number 18 is _____

16. The mental peg for number 9 is _____

17. The mental peg for number 14 is _____

18. The mental peg for number 11 is _____

19. The mental peg for number 4 is _____

20. The mental peg for number 1 is _____

Your Total Score: _____

*(Answers: dime, ladder, star, octopus, magazine, clock, tricycle, pirate, fingers and toes, heaven, lips, golf club, shoe, six-shooter, 18-wheeler, cat, heart, skis, compass, penny)*

If you were able to accurately name every mental peg above, your Virtual Peg Board is locked into your memory. If however, you missed one or more answers (or could not easily recall any of the pegs) you need to review Steps 1 and 2 and retake the test before reading further in this book.

## Using Memory as a Springboard for Intuition

If you're like most people, you probably found this workshop to be incredibly easy because of the intuitive associations between the objects in the garage and the numbers 1 through 20.  And you thought memorizing was hard work! Well memorizing is hard work. But we're not memorizing here, we're connecting you to a body of knowledge you already have in the intellectual memory of your left and right brain and the emotional memory of your body.

This is holistic memory—the left brain, the right brain and the body. The memory processes of the Link, the Loci and the Peg work in harmony with your mind and body to dramatically increase your ability to record, retain and retrieve information. You accomplish this by making a crystal clear vivid mental image of that information, sealing in that memory trace with emotions, and reconnecting to the information through your mental command system of access routes.

The more senses you record a memory with, the more access routes you open and collectively these access routes become linked as bridges within the mind-body information highway. These access routes and information bridges although organized in free-flowing categories are dynamic; continually networking and reconnecting to create new memory maps.

This memory rich environment is where the ideas of tomorrow's successes are born. At present these seed memories are loosely floating but in an instant can be connected with other newly formed ideas to generate inspiration and streams of new thinking. This is the promise of a multi-dimensional architecture of memory *holographically stored and transmitted in an instant of a milli-second...*as when light touches one facet of a crystal and immediately illuminates the rest.

This is you lighting up. The sudden rush of insight and knowing as your mind and body process the patterns of *what it knows* from past experience against *what it is receiving* from incoming data and stimuli. This is not memorizing. You don't need to memorize. You simply need to make a connection—a connection, as with the Peg System, to a mental peg where you can hang new items of information.

In the next upcoming *Photographic Mind Workshop*, you will participate in a challenging and exciting memory task that asks you to solve a Murder Mystery Party whose outcome will amaze you with your incredible ability of recall as you put the power of the Peg System to work for you.

## Activating Your Virtual Peg Board

In the previous *Photographic Mind Workshop* you locked the Peg System into your memory by permanently hanging your 20 mental pegs onto your Virtual Peg Board. The way you did that was through easily recognizable associations between the 20 picture-words with the numbers 1 through 20. These mental pegs give you 20 new locations to file, organize and hang incoming information so that you know where to look to find that information to boost your memory power.

Like the Chain and Loci Systems, the Peg System allows for the sequential storage of information, but even better, the Peg System lets you directly access any specific numbered information item without needing to run through the items coming either before it or after it. In the next upcoming *Photographic Mind*

*Workshop* you will activate your Virtual Peg Board by learning how to hang information from each of the pegs and then experience the power of your Peg Board in a live memory task.

## How to Hang Information on Your Virtual Peg Board

The process you use to hang items on your Virtual Peg Board is the same process you used for both the Link and the Loci Systems. As you recall, it consists of two phases:

1. Create a mental picture of your peg word and the item to be hung onto the peg.
2. Put the two together in a crazy, illogical, bizarre way and lock in that mental image with emotion.

All the techniques you used to visualize your mental images with the Link and Loci Systems apply equally as well to the Peg System. Use action, exaggeration, and quantity to engage your intellectual memory. Involve all your senses to bring in your emotional memory, and put yourself in the picture as well. Remember, you want vivid mental pictures, full of clarity and descriptive detail.

## You're Invited to a Murder Mystery Party!

To prepare you for the upcoming *Photographic Mind Workshop*, imagine you are a guest at a party. The party is focused around a murder mystery event which has a total of 20 clues for the evidence consisting of 7 weapons, 6 suspects, and 7 locations.

The Murder Mystery Party gets underway by introducing all the possible crime evidence. You are first allowed to inspect the 7 possible murder weapons. Then you read the dossiers of the 6 possible suspects. Lastly, you are shown photographs of the 7 locations where the crime might have been committed.

After presenting all the possible evidence—the 7 weapons, the 6 suspects, and the 7 photograph locations—all the evidence is whisked away. You are told that after an hour has passed, you will be presented once again with all the weapons, dossiers, and locations—*with one minor difference.* <u>There will be one weapon, one dossier and one location left out. Your challenge is to identify these missing pieces of evidence and thereby solve the murder mystery</u>.

The first party guest to correctly identify the correct weapon, suspect, and location will be the winner...and walk away with $2,000. The rules are deceivingly simple though, the catch here is that no one is allowed to use a pencil and paper to record the clues before or after the presenting of evidence.

Most people would walk away from this challenge—and the $2,000—feeling hopeless. But not you. *You have the beautiful system for recording all the clues instantly, easily and permanently—whether that information needs to be recalled in one hour or one month.* For you have the Peg System at your command.

## Photographic Mind Workshop: The Murder Mystery Party

### Step 1: Active Learning Session

**To enhance your experience of the material please play the** ***Accelerated Learning Music*** **soundtrack (located on Track #2 of your** ***Brain Supercharger*** **CD) while you complete the following workshop exercise.**

In this session you will participate in an interactive learning process that shows you how to hang the weapons, suspects and crime locations onto your Virtual Peg Board. By comparing your Virtual Peg Board to the evidence presented at the end of the party, you will easily be able to recall the missing items and win the $2,000.

As you read along, let your imagination play with the crazy, illogical, bizarre pictures you see and use your emotions to lock the pieces of evidence onto your Virtual Peg Board.

A little further into the session you'll verbalize—out loud—the phrases that describe how each item is hanging on a mental peg.

## • Presenting the Weapons

The 7 weapons all have numbered ID tags attached. They are as follows: number 1 is a candlestick, number 2 is an iron, number 3 is an ax, number 4 is a rope, number 5 is a knife, number 6 is a pillow (for suffocating) and the last one, number 7 is a bottle of sleeping pills. The first seven mental pegs are PENNY, SHOES, TRICYCLE, COMPASS, STAR, 6-SHOOTER and HEAVEN. Visually hanging each item on the corresponding peg you can imagine the following:

*A **candle** dripping melted <u>pennies</u> onto your stomach burning your skin.*

*Your mother **iron**ing your <u>shoes</u> as you walk out the door.*

*An **ax** hacking up a <u>tricycle</u> with all the pieces turning into new tricycles.*

*A **rope** strangling the <u>compass</u> making the needle go around and around.*

*A <u>star</u> hurling many **knives** into the moon who is crying.*

*Your **bed pillow** stuffed with <u>6-shooters</u> that are continually shooting bullets at your head as you try to sleep.*

*Angels in <u>heaven</u> flying on **sleeping pills** like witches on broomsticks.*

Are you getting the picture here? The mental images you create here are scenes that could never happen in real life and they are imbued with emotion. Remember to use exaggeration, adding quantity, action, and using your senses to involve yourself in the picture as much as possible. Create crazy, illogical and bizarre images—and then lock them in with emotion.

### • Presenting the Suspects

The next six bits of crime evidence are the suspects—Dr. Wells, Professor Caswell, Mrs. Monarch, Senator Maroni, Mrs. Lyons, and Ms. Berg. The next six mental pegs are OCTOPUS, CAT, DIME, SKIS, CLOCK and LADDER.

Before we peg each suspect, you need to turn these names into concrete pictures that you can easily visualize and hang on your mental pegs. We covered this idea of "word substitution" in the last workshop where you used the easily visualized pictures of HEAVEN and PIRATE as symbols for the intangible associations of 7th HEAVEN and 15 MEN ON A DEAD MAN'S CHEST. In this workshop you'll use another technique of word substitution which uses a sound alike word to represent the word you are trying to memorize.

For example, the second suspect is Professor Caswell. You can't picture a Caswell, but you can picture a CASTLE, which sounds very similar to CASWELL. Therefore you use a CASTLE to represent this suspect, and your true memory will fill in the right letters when you need to recall the name. Visually hanging each suspect onto the corresponding peg you can see the following image for each suspect:

DR. WELLS: *A gigantic <u>octopus</u> grabbing all the money you throw into a*

*wishing **well**.*

PROFESSOR CASWELL: *Garfield (<u>the cat</u>) hanging for dear life on the high*

*wall of a **castle**.*

MRS. MONARCH: *A **monarch** butterfly depositing <u>dimes</u> in a parking meter.*

SENATOR MARONI: *A bowl of **macaroni** flying down the mountain on a*

*pair of <u>skis</u>.*

MRS. LYONS: *A **lion** wearing wrist <u>watches</u> on all his legs.*

MRS. BERG: *A series of ice**bergs** connected to each other with <u>ladders</u>.*

If you are having difficulty with any of these ask yourself *"Do I know my Virtual Peg Board?"* and *"Is my visual mental picture of the suspect as hung on the mental peg memorable?"* If you can remember your Peg Board, but you can't see the suspect, you need to beef up your mental image with exaggeration, quantity, action—be sure to use your senses and/or involve yourself in the picture.

### • Presenting the 7 Crime Locations

The remaining pieces of evidence are the 7 crime location photographs which are a football stadium, a post office, a cemetery, a coffee shop, a library, a museum of natural history and a car dealership.

Your last seven mental pegs are HEART, PIRATE, LIPS, MAGAZINE, 18-WHEELER, GOLF CLUB, and finally, FINGERS and TOES. Visually hanging each crime location on the corresponding mental peg you can see:

*A football team of <u>hearts</u> running around the **football stadium**.*

*A <u>pirate</u> slashing open your mailbox (symbolizing the **post office**) as you reach inside to get your mail.*

*A **cemetery** full of tombstones made of <u>lips</u>, with each one speaking the name of the deceased in the grave.*

*A **coffee pot** (symbolizing the **coffee shop**) made out of a cover of a <u>magazine</u> pouring coffee on top of your head.*

*An <u>18-wheeler</u> in the sky pulling a **library**, like Santa's reindeer pull the sled.*

*A **dinosaur** (symbolizing the **museum of natural history**) playing <u>golf</u>.*

*See your <u>toes and fingers</u> surfing on the hood of a red sports car*

*(symbolizing the **car dealership**).*

## Chunking the Descriptive Phrases

Were you able to vividly see these images? Can you feel your brain connecting the evidence to your Virtual Peg Board and then searching for the number association? If all this is a little hazy to you now, know that it will become clearer with practice.

Let's hang the 20 pieces of evidence a second time. This time, you'll chunk the phrases describing the way each item is hung onto your Virtual Peg Board. Be sure to verbalize the phrases out loud to increase your power of recall.

As you say the phrases, remember to feel the action. Engage your intellectual memory through the devices of exaggeration and quantity. And put yourself into the picture—hear the 6-shooters firing in your pillow, feel the pirate slash out at you as you reach for your mail, and laugh at the sight of your fingers and toes surfing over the hood of that red car.

Please recite (out loud) the following chunked descriptive phrases.

### • Hanging the Seven Weapons

A **candle** dripping melted <u>pennies</u> onto your stomach burning your skin.

Your mother **iron**ing your <u>shoes</u> as you walk out the door.

An **ax** hacking up a <u>tricycle</u> with all the pieces turning into new tricycles.

A **rope** strangling the <u>compass</u> making the needle go around and around.

A <u>star</u> hurling many **knives** into the moon who is crying.

Your **bed pillow** stuffed with <u>6-shooters</u> that are continually shooting bullets at your head as you try to sleep.

Angels in <u>heaven</u> flying on **sleeping pills** like witches on broomsticks.

### • Hanging the Six Suspects

DR. WELLS: A gigantic <u>octopus</u> grabbing all the money you throw into a wishing **well**.

PROFESSOR CASWELL: Garfield (<u>the cat</u>) hanging for dear life on the high wall of a **castle**.

MRS. MONARCH: A **monarch** butterfly depositing <u>dimes</u> in a parking meter.

SENATOR MARONI: A bowl of **macaroni** flying down the mountain on a pair of <u>skis</u>.

MRS. LYONS: A **lion** wearing wrist <u>watches</u> on all his legs.

MRS. BERG: A series of ice**bergs** connected to each other with <u>ladders</u>.

- **Hanging the Seven Crime Locations**

  A football team of <u>hearts</u> running around the **football stadium**.

  A <u>pirate</u> slashing open your mailbox (symbolizing the **post office**) as you reach inside to get your mail.

  A **cemetery** full of tombstones made of <u>lips</u>, with each one speaking the name of the deceased in the grave.

  A **coffee pot** (symbolizing the **coffee shop**) made out of a cover of a <u>magazine</u> pouring coffee on top of your head.

  An <u>18-wheeler</u> in the sky pulling a **library**, like Santa's reindeer pull the sled.

  A **dinosaur** (symbolizing the museum of **natural history**) playing <u>golf</u>.

  See your <u>toes and fingers</u> surfing on the hood of a red sports car (symbolizing the **car dealership**).

## Step 2: Passive Learning Session

The hanging of the 20 pieces of evidence onto your Virtual Peg Board as learned in the Active Learning Session is illustrated on the next page without the use of any words. Spend the next two minutes gazing at this scene. As this session is designed for unconscious learning, allowing your mind to wander will give you the maximum benefit. Try not to concentrate on any one element you see.

As you see each image, let all your emotions come into play. See the hilarity of your mother ironing your shoes as you walk out the door, imagine hundreds of butterflies descending onto a parking lot with dimes on their wings, hear the eerie way the tombstones speak the names of the deceased.

While it is not necessary for you to see these in the order in which they were presented, realize that your mind intuitively knows the order based on the association in your memory. For example, you should know that Mr. Caswell (represented by _____ hanging onto the_____) was the (4th?, 7th? 9th? 11th?) piece of evidence presented. That answer is 9th. The reason you know this is because of the association between CAT and NINE LIVES. As you relax and open your mind to the whole scene don't be surprised when the order of the evidence presented simply pops into your mind.

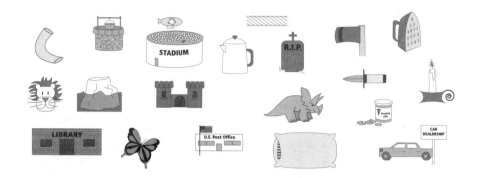

To help lock-in your lesson please play the *Super Memory Transformation* Soundtrack (located on Track #3 of your *Brain Supercharger* CD). Put the book aside for now and make sure to use stereo headphones. Find a comfortable position & quiet place where you can rest undisturbed for the next 30 minutes.

## Step 3: Assessment

The Murder Mystery Party is almost over. As promised, the evidence is returned for your viewing, except of course for the three pieces of evidence that were involved in the crime. The guest who can correctly identify these three pieces of missing evidence will win the $2,000 prize.

You see 5 of the 6 suspect dossiers. You see 7 of the 8 crime locations. But wait—there are no weapons—only their ID tags. *Where are the weapons?* You and the other guests are told that tragically, the crime officer who was in charge of watching over the evidence is now missing, and all the weapons are gone too. *All that's left behind are the weapons' ID tags. The only way to identify the weapon is to remember which weapon went with what numbered ID tag.* But that should be easy for you!

Using your Virtual Peg Board, identify the missing weapon, missing suspect dossier and the missing photograph of the crime location. When you are done, compare your list to the answers provided and write your total number of correct answers on the score line (each correct answer is worth one point).

## Returned Weapon ID Tags

No. 7, No. 3, No. 2, No. 4, No. 1, No. 6

## Returned Suspect Dossiers

Dr. Wells

Professor Caswell

Mrs. Monarch

Mrs. Lyons

Mrs. Berg

## Returned Photos of Crime Locations

Football stadium

Post office

Cemetery

Library

Museum of natural history

Car dealership

## Solve the Murder by Identifying the Correct Evidence

The weapon was: _____

The suspect was: _____

The location was: _____

Your Total Score: _____

*(Answers: The missing weapon was the knife. The missing suspect was Senator Marconi. And the missing photograph of the crime location was the coffee shop.)*

Did you win the $2,000 prize? If not, ask yourself these two questions:

- *Do I know the mental pegs?* If not, practice recalling the pegs by the association that connects them with a specific number.

• *Can I see the piece of evidence hanging on my Virtual Peg Board?* If not, try hanging it on your prop a different way than as told in the story.

For example, if you can't remember the coffee pot as being a magazine, connect the two in a different way. Imagine going to your cupboard in the morning (or wherever you keep your coffee) and see your familiar coffee bag (or jar) jump out at you holding an issue of Seventeen Magazine. Hear it laugh at you because you're not 17 any more and need to have a cup of coffee to get going in the morning! Remember to bring in your emotions through your senses. Make these connections crystal clear in your mind. When you do, every piece of evidence will simply pop into your memory as quickly and easily as the pictures on your Virtual Peg Board.

Again, the mind sees in pictures. Plus, the mind does not forget what it creates. You created your Virtual Peg Board by building on the intuitive associations you had in your mind to the items in the garage. The Peg System works because it is a natural extension of how your mind and body remembers— through pictures, through associations, through chunking, through emotions.

If you did not win the $2,000 prize, review Steps 1 and 2 and then create your own Murder Mystery Party. Simply write the numbers of the 6 weapons and the names of the 7 suspects and crime locations on pieces of paper. Then turn each over and pull out one weapon, one suspect and one crime location. Keeping these three pieces aside, turn over all the other evidence and see how fast you can come up with the three missing pieces of evidence.

## Connecting to the Power of Information

This Murder Mystery Party was a true story—except for the money part! Over 40 people were invited to the party. And the first to solve the murder came up with the answer in under 2 minutes. How did she do it? She used the Peg System—it was a different version from yours, but it was a Peg System none the less. Everybody at the party was amazed by her memory power.

The fact is, when you use these powerful memory systems, you'll amaze everyone—your peers and the higher-ups as well. *Not simply because you can remember things, but because you can make quick informed decisions due to the fact that the information you need to make those knowledgeable decisions is right there in your head and not buried in a report in a file cabinet.*

An often overlooked benefit of this course is simply this: while other people are preoccupied with the busyness of the information load, *you are simply taking it all in*, mentally linking and patterning the incoming information with something already in your mind through the maps created by your intellectual and emotional memory. As a result, you have at your mental fingertips the information that others need minutes, hours, or even days to find.

With the Link or Loci System, for example, you can recall a list of 20 competing products, or 20 vendors, or 20 cities where you have branch locations. With the Peg System you can carry a timeline of your company's products right in your head, or the rank order of the top 20 salespeople on your team, or know which are the 20 worst performing stocks of the day.

The bottom line here is that regardless of the field you are in, you need to connect with information every minute of everyday to excel in whatever it is that you do. The Link, the Loci, and the Peg Systems are powerful processes that will let you connect to this information with ease. Yet even more powerful than these is the next memory system—the Phonetic.

# The Phonetic System

In the first six workshops of this program you have learned three different systems—the Link, the Loci and the Peg. Through the use of all these systems you can recall 60 to 80 items rather easily. And while that is not an insignificant amount of data to be able to record, retain and retrieve, you still need to expand your memory capability beyond this boundary. With the next system you can. It is called the Phonetic System. *And it is the most powerful memory system of all.*

With the Phonetic System you can remember credit card numbers, social security numbers, license plate numbers, statistics, formulas, prices, dates, as well as lists.

This system has been around for over 300 years. It is virtually limitless. And best of all, it is easy to understand. This ingenious system uses 10 consonant sounds, or letters to represent the digits 0 through 9. The consonant sounds allow you to code the numbers you need to remember into words, which are more meaningful and thus easier to remember than the numbers themselves. This principle is the same one used behind toll free telephone numbers which use a word instead of digits to help you recall their phone number.

## The Genius of the Phonetic Code

Just as with the pegs on your Virtual Peg Board, there is an association you can make in the Phonetic Code between the number and the consonant sound so that the code is easy to learn.

For example, the Phonetic Code for the number 2 is the "n" sound, represented by the lower case letter "n." Before reading on, ask yourself "What could be the association that connects the number 2 to the 'n'? " A helpful hint is in knowing that the Phonetic Code for the 3 is a lower case "m." Can you see the pattern here? The reason why 2 is represented by a lower case "n" is the same reason for the 3 being represented with a lower case "m." And both answers have to do with the shape of the letter.

Do you see this association? <u>The association is in the number of down strokes each letter has</u>. *The "n" has two down strokes and the "m" has three down strokes*. Again, it is important to remember that these are lower case letters. In the Phonetic System, the 2 is represented by the "n" sound, and the 3 is represented by the "m" sound.

There are 8 other digits and corresponding sounds in the Phonetic System. Most numbers represent more than one consonant. However, the reason for this is that the number represents a consonant <u>sound</u>, and not just a consonant <u>letter</u>.

For example, the number 1 could be represented by either a "t" or a "d." <u>These letters are grouped together because they have a similar consonant sound</u>. And they have a similar consonant sound because your mouth and tongue are in a similar position when making each of those sounds.

To prove it to yourself say the words <u>T</u>WO and <u>D</u>REW and pay close attention to how you form those words. Your tongue is on the roof of your mouth—right behind your teeth—for both sounds. The "t" and "d" are both said to be in the <u>same family of sounds, meaning they both sound somewhat alike</u>. In the Phonetic System that family of sounds is represented by the number 1. Why the number 1? *Because the "t" has only one down stroke—the association here is through the shape of the "t."*

It is easy to see the association graphically between the number 1 and the "t" and once you understand the concept of the "family of sounds" between the "t" and the "d" it is easy to understand how these 2 letters can be represented by one consonant sound.

Again, what is important in this system is the consonant sound represented by each of the 10 numbers—rather than a *specific letter*. To learn how to use this system for recalling numbers of any length, you simply need to know the Phonetic Code, which gives you the consonant sound for the numbers 0 through 9, and some simple guidelines that will let you code your numbers into words. In the upcoming *Photographic Mind Workshop* you will learn the remainder of the

Phonetic code by seeing the association between the consonant sounds and the digits 0 through 9 that they represent.

## Photographic Mind Workshop: Cracking the Phonetic Code

### Step 1: Active Learning Session

**To enhance your experience of the material please play the _Accelerated Learning Music_ soundtrack (located on Track #2 of your _Brain Supercharger_ CD) while you complete the following workshop exercise.**

During this step you will follow along in your book as you learn the Phonetic Code, which pairs up the consonant sounds with the digits 0 through 9, and the association that links each one. As you read each one, it is important that you look for the association between the number and the consonant sound.

What you're creating here is a memory map on how 10 sounds are linked with 10 numbers. All you're doing is taking that which you already know (the numbers, the letters, and their sounds) and organizing it in a new way based on the pattern found in the association—as with 2 is to "n" and 3 is to "m" because of the number of down stokes in the letter.

Just as with the mental pegs on your Virtual Peg Board, the associations are intuitive once you discover the pattern. You will find that it takes less time to understand the Phonetic Code than it takes to explain it because, as you learned in Part I, your brain is a master at finding patterns.

A little further into the session you'll hear the Phonetic Code again, only this time you'll be asked to verbalize out loud the numbers, their consonant sounds and the association that connects the two. The powerful sensory triad of seeing, reading, and verbalizing the material will have you memorizing at an accelerated rate.

The following guidelines describe the Phonetic Code and the associations that will allow you to recall the sounds represented by each digit.

*Number 1 represents the consonant sound of "t and d." I can remember 1 because "t" has one down stroke in it.*

*Number 2 represents the consonant sound of "n." I can remember 2 because "n" has 2 down strokes in it.*

*Number 3 represents the consonant sound of "m." I can remember 3 because "m" has 3 down strokes in it.*

*Number 4 represents the consonant sound of "r." I can remember 4 because "r" is the last letter in four.*

*Number 5 represents the consonant sound of "L." I can remember 5 because when I spread the 5 fingers of my left hand (its back facing me) I can see an "L" made by the thumb and forefinger.*

*Number 6 represents the consonant sound of "j, sh, ch, dg, and soft g." I can hear this sound in the words JOT, SHOP, CHOP, GRUDGE, and GEM. I can remember 6 because "j" and 6 are almost mirror images.*

*Number 7 represents the consonant sound of "k, q, hard c, and hard g." I can hear this sound in the words KELP, QUELL, CUT, and GUT. I can remember 7 because "K" looks like two 7s.*

*Number 8 represents the consonant sound of "f and v." I can remember 8 because a lower case script "f" looks like an 8.*

*Number 9 represents the consonant sound of "b and p." I can remember 9 because "p" is a mirror image to 9.*

*The number 0 represents the consonant sound of "z, s, and soft c." I can remember 0 because there is a "z" in zero.*

Are you seeing the association made here between the number and the consonant sound? And can you grasp the reason why some numbers can be represented by more than one letter? To help this become clearer in your mind, <u>listen intently to the similarities between the consonant sounds in each family</u>. It will become clearer as you give it some more practice.

## Chunking the Phonetic Code

Now that you understand the connection between the number and the letters/consonants it represents, you can use the chart on the next page to graphically summarize the code quickly and easily.

The chart has three columns. The first column shows the digits, the second column shows the consonant sounds and letters the digit represents, and the third column tells you the association linking the digit with its consonant sound and letter. Moving across the chart from left to right read the digit (in the first column, say out loud the consonant sound and letters represented by the digit (in the second column) and use the association (in the third column) to lock this information into your mind.

Pay attention to the way your tongue, teeth and lips move to form the shape that produces the sound. This is a movement that becomes locked into your memory. Pay attention to these letters as you say them and discover the similarities they share.

As you say each line, mentally click with the association that connects the number to the letters/consonant sounds. Take your time. At this point, speed is not important. The goal is to see the pattern of the code through the associations.

| Digit | Consonant Sound & Letters | The Association |
|-------|---------------------------|----------------|
| 1 | t, d | The "t" has one downstroke. |
| 2 | n | The "n" has 2 downstrokes. |
| 3 | m | The "m" has 3 downstrokes. |
| 4 | r | Four ends in "r." |
| 5 | l | Thumb and forefinger make the shape of an "L" when 5 fingers spread out. |
| 6 | j, sh, ch, dg, soft g | Capital "J" is mirror image to 6. |
| 7 | k, q, hard c, hard g | Capital "K" looks like two 7s put together. |
| 8 | f, v | Cursive "f" looks like an 8. |
| 9 | b, p | "P" is a mirror image to 9. |
| 0 | z, s, soft c | First sound in the word zero is "z." |

Number 1 represents the consonant sound of "t and d." I can remember 1 because "t" has one down stroke in it.

Number 2 represents the consonant sound of "n." I can remember 2 because "n" has 2 down strokes in it.

Number 3 represents the consonant sound of "m." I can remember 3 because "m" has 3 down strokes in it.

Number 4 represents the consonant sound of "r." I can remember 4 because "r" is the last letter in four.

Number 5 represents the consonant sound of "L." I can remember 5 because when I spread the 5 fingers of my left hand (its back facing me) I can see an "L" made by the thumb and forefinger.

Number 6 represents the consonant sound of "j, sh, ch, dg, and soft g." I can hear this sound in the words JOT, SHOP, CHOP, GRUDGE, and GEM. I can remember 6 because "j" and 6 are almost mirror images.

Number 7 represents the consonant sound of "k, q, hard c, and hard g." I can hear this sound in the words KELP, QUELL, CUT, and GUT. I can remember 7 because "K" looks like two 7s.

Number 8 represents the consonant sound of "f and v." I can remember 8 because a lower case script "f" looks like an 8.

Number 9 represents the consonant sound of "b and p." I can remember 9 because "p" is a mirror image to 9.

The number 0 represents the consonant sound of "z, s, and soft c." I can remember 0 because there is a "z" in zero.

That is the whole Phonetic System—just 10 numbers and 10 consonant sounds. These are all you need to know to code any string of abstract numbers into concrete words that you can then picture with images to lock the number into your mind.

## Step 2: Passive Learning Session

The numbers, consonant sounds/letters and the associations of the Phonetic Code that you learned in the Active Learning Session are shown below with visuals. Spend the next two minutes gazing at them. As this session is designed for unconscious learning, allowing your mind to wander will give you the maximum benefit. Try not to concentrate on any one item that you see.

As your eyes see the visuals, feel the association pop into your mind that connects the number to the letters/consonants. It is not necessary to do these in any order because your mind intuitively knows the order based on the association in your memory. Just relax and let your mind open as you sweep through the whole scene and recall the code.

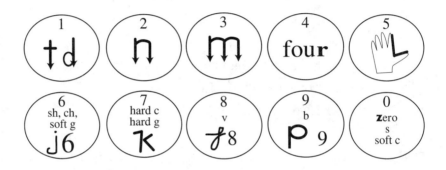

To help lock-in your lesson please play the *Super Memory Transformation* Soundtrack (located on Track #3 of your *Brain Supercharger* CD). Put the book aside for now and make sure to use stereo headphones. Find a comfortable position & quiet place where you can rest undisturbed for the next 30 minutes.

## Step 3: Assessment

The next workshop gives you the opportunity to try out this memory system, but before you can move on, you need to demonstrate your ability to remember the Phonetic Code easily and accurately.

Please write the letters/consonant sounds for each number. After you are done, compare your list to the answers provided and write your total number of correct answers on the score line. Each letter (or pair of letters, such as "sh," "ch") count as one point.

**Phonetic Code Recall**

| Digit | Consonant Sound & Letters |
|-------|---------------------------|
| 1 | |
| 2 | |
| 3 | |
| 4 | |
| 5 | |
| 6 | |
| 7 | |
| 8 | |
| 9 | |
| 0 | |

Your Total Score: _____

*(Answers: 1 = t, d  2 = n  3 = m  4 = r  5 = l  6 = j, sh, ch, dg, soft s 7 = k, g, hard c, hard g  8 = f, v  9 = b, p  0 = z, s, soft c)*

By now you should feel very confident of your knowledge of the phonetic code. You should be able to recite the consonant sound and letters that go with each number as well as be able to identify the number that goes with the consonant sounds and letters. If you remembered all of the consonant sounds and letters in the chart (for a total of 22 points) you are ready to continue on in the book. If however, the Phonetic Code is not firmly implanted in your memory, please review Steps 1 and 2 and retake the test before reading on.

## The Five Rules of the Phonetic Code

Just as there were ground rules to working with the Loci System, there are ground rules for applying the Phonetic Code. Once you learn these, you can begin to apply the Phonetic System to see exactly how it works.

- **The first rule is that the vowels a, e, i, o, and u have no numerical value.**
- **The second rule is that the letters w, h, and y also have no numerical value.** (These spell the word "why" so they are easy to remember.)
- **The third rule is that silent letters have no value.** For example, the letter "b" in dumb is silent, therefore it is disregarded.
- **The fourth rule is that double letters (which produce the same sound) only count once.** For example, the word "summer" contains the letter "m" twice but you only hear one of them. In the word "summer," only the first "m" would receive a number code. On the other hand, "accident" has two "c"s but each "c" is pronounced differently—the first "c" is hard but the second "c" is soft. In the word "accident" both "c"s would receive a numerical code.
- **The fifth rule is that the letter "x" is coded according to the way it sounds.** For example, in the word "ax" the "x" sounds like a "ks" so it would get two numbers—a number for "k" and a number for "s." On the other hand, with the word "complexion" the "x" sounds like "ksh." Therefore it would get the number for "k" and the number for "sh."

With the use of these rules the Phonetic System becomes the most powerful memory system in this course. Unlike the other three systems, it is ideal for remembering long strings of numbers, which being abstract information, are the hardest of all to remember.

## Coding Words into Numbers

An easy way to start with the Phonetic Code is by translating short words into their code numbers. The first word we'll try is BAG. <u>Say the word and listen to only the consonants—remember, the vowels are not coded into numbers.</u>

The first consonant sound you hear is a B sound. This sound is represented by the number 9. The second consonant sound you hear is a G sound. This is a "hard g" and receives the number 7. The word BAG, then, gets the code of 97.

Now try the word TIE. The first consonant sound is T. This sound is represented by the number 1. <u>It is also the only letter in this word to receive a code because the other two letters are vowels which receive no numerical code.</u> So TIE is simply represented by the number 1.

How about the word RYE? The R sound receives a 4. And the letters Y and E don't receive a numerical value because they are vowels. The word RYE then is simply represented by the number 4.

Now let's move on to a larger word, SUMMER. The S sound gets a 0. You ignore the U because it is a vowel. The first M gets what number? Remember the association of the number of down strokes? The M gets a number 3. <u>The second M is ignored, because of the rule which states that double consonants which have the same sound do not count.</u> Then you skip over the E again because it is a vowel. This leads you to the last sound of R, and this receives a 4—because 4 ends in R. The word SUMMER then would be 034.

As you go through these words, remember that the Phonetic System is based on the consonant <u>sound</u>—and not on the letter itself. Different letters or combinations of letters can take on the same sounds. For example, the "sh" sound can be made by the letter S, as in <u>S</u>UGAR, or the letter C as in O<u>C</u>EAN, or the letters CI as in GRA<u>CI</u>OUS, or the letters TI as in RA<u>TI</u>O or even the letters TION as in VACA<u>TION</u>. All of these letters or letter combinations would be represented by the number 6.

## Turning Numbers into Words

Now that you've seen how to put words into numbers, let's do the opposite and code numbers into words. After you get the hang of it, the Phonetic System is almost contagious. You'll find yourself automatically turning every number into a word.

Turning a number into a word is an easy 3-step process:

1. Translate each digit of the number into a letter using the numerical code.
2. Build words from the letters by adding the non-numerical letters which are the vowels and the letters W, H, and Y.
3. Use the link system to connect these words and then lock these crazy, illogical, bizarre mental images into your memory with your emotions.

## Photographic Mind Workshop: A Baker's Dozen

### Step 1: Active Learning Session

**To enhance your experience of the material please play the *Accelerated Learning Music* soundtrack (located on Track #2 of your *Brain Supercharger* CD) while you complete the following workshop exercise.**

Imagine you own a small and bustling bakery in a summer resort. Every morning you are the first eatery open and people are lining the sidewalk to get into your door for their doughnut and coffee. All the doughnuts in your shop are freshly made, and each batch is precisely mixed and baked by a computer based on a unique 13-digit code you enter into its memory.

Because this code is the secret to your success, you do not want to write it down and take the chance that an employee in your shop would take your special formula to another bakery. Your only alternative is to memorize the code.

During this step you will follow along in your book as you apply the three steps of the Phonetic Code to turn this 13-digit number into a silly phrase that will allow you to recall the number. As you read the material, focus on the associations that you learned from the Phonetic Code that connect each number to its consonant sounds/letters. A little further into the session you'll verbalize out loud the process you followed to create the word phrase for the 13-digit number.

The unique 13-digit code that you program every morning into the computer is: 7280251023945.

**Step 1: Translate each digit of the number into a letter using the phonetic code.**

Working with the first 3-digits, you could choose a C for the 7, pick-up the N for the 2, and choose an F for the 8—for the letters CNF.

Now, taking the next 5 numbers of 02510, you could take an S for the 0, pick-up the N for the 2, pick-up the L for the 5, choose the D for the 1 and an S for the 0. This would give you the letters SNLDS.

The remaining numbers are 23945. The 2 becomes an N, the 3 becomes an M, you could choose a B for the 9, the 4 becomes an R and the 5 becomes an L—resulting in the letters NMBRL.

By the end of Step 1 you would have CNFSNLDSNMBRL.

**Step 2: Build words from the letters by adding the non-numerical letters which are the vowels and the letters W, H, and Y.**

There is no set way you need to chunk the letters into words. For ease, it was arbitrarily broken up into three sets of letters. And the first set has 3 letters: CNF. Adding the non-numerical vowels to these first three letters could form the words "a CaN oF" as shown below.

```
code:  7  2  8     0  2  5  1  0  2  3  9  4  5
       C  N  F
     a CaN oF
```

The next string of numbers translated into SNLDS. Adding the non-numerical vowels could form the words "SuN hoLDS" as shown on the next page.

```
code:  7  2  8      0  2      5  1  0        2  3  9  4  5
       C  N  F      S  N      L  D  S
      a CaN oF      SuN       hoLDS
```

The last string of numbers translated into NMBRL. Now, adding the non-numerical letters to this last chunk, you could form the words "aN uMBRELla," as shown below.

```
code:  7  2  8      0  2      5  1  0      2        3  9  4  5
       C  N  F      S  N      L  D  S      N        M  B  R  L
      a CaN oF      SuN       hoLDS       aN        uMBReLla
```

This phrase is possible because of the letters that do no receive a number: the vowels, the letters WHY or any double letters which produce the same sound (as with the two "l"s in "umbrella.")

**Step 3: Use the link system to connect these words and then lock these crazy, illogical, bizarre mental images into your memory with your emotions.** Our total word phrase then is "a CaN oF SuN hoLDS aN uMBRELla."

To recall the 13-digit number all you need to do is think of the first word in the link, CaN, and translate it back into digits 72. This takes you to the oF which translates into 8. This leads you to SuN, and this translates into 02. SuN would then remind you of hoLDS aN MBReLla which translates to 51023945. Put it all together and you have your secret formula code of 7280251023945.

## A Storyboard of Your Link Phrase

The more you work with this process, the easier it will become for you. The above example took you through the process step-by-step to arrive at the link phrase. Let's repeat this again—only this time you'll do Steps 1, 2 and 3 nearly simultaneously on each chunk.

The chart is accompanied by a storyboard that acts out the process you went through to code the number into a six word link. It is followed by the actual statements of how you arrived at each word. Read the following statements out loud as you look at your storyboard and chart that illustrate your process. Be sure to verbalize the phrases out loud to increase your power of recall.

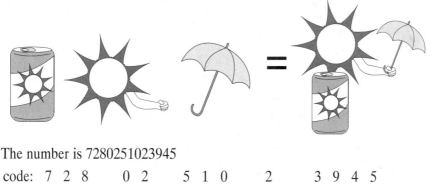

The number is 7280251023945

code:  7  2  8      0  2      5  1  0      2      3  9  4  5
       C  N  F      S  N      L  D  S      N      M  B  R  L
      a CaN oF      SuN       hoLDS       aN      uMBReLla

Working with the first 3-digits a C was chosen for the 7, an N was chosen for the 2, and an F chosen for the 8. Adding non-numerical letters with the Phonetic Code formed the words "a CaN oF."

Taking the next 5 numbers an S was chosen for the 0, an N was picked-up for the 2, L was chosen for the 5, D was chosen for the 1, and an S chosen for the 0. Adding non-numerical letters with the Phonetic Code formed the words "SuN hoLDS."

In the remaining 5 numbers, the 2 became an N, the 3 became an M, B was chosen for the 9, the 4 became an R, and the 5 became an L. Now, adding non-numerical letters to the Phonetic Code translated these letters into "aN uMBRELla."

The resulting phonetic word phrase is "a CaN oF SuN hoLDS aN uMBRELla."

Did you feel your brain jumping through the process this time? The first time you coded this number you were probably nearly lost beyond belief, as if you were reading a foreign language. In reality, the Phonetic Code is a new language yet it is made up of elements you already know. Just as the same letters of the alphabet can be re-configured in English, Spanish or French these same consonant sounds/letters and numbers can be re-configured in English to connect you with a new way of thinking. And just as with learning a foreign language, the more you speak it, the more automatic it becomes.

The Phonetic System is like a secret language—a language that invites you to explore a whole new world of memory power. Although this may be the harder of the four memory systems to learn initially, once mastered it opens up a new universe of possibilities.

## Step 2: Passive Learning Session

The storyboard below visualizes the process you went through to code the 13- digit number into the link "a CaN oF SuN hoLDS aN uMBRELla."

Spend the next two minutes gazing at the images. As this session is designed for unconscious learning, allowing your mind to wander will give you the maximum benefit. Try not to concentrate on any one item that you see.

As your eyes see the visuals, feel the process working backwards in your mind allowing you to decode the letters back into the numbers. As you do, let the association pop into your mind that connects the consonant sound/letter to the number. Your mind intuitively knows these connections. You are now locking these memory maps into place. Just relax and let your mind open as you sweep through the whole scene and recall the code.

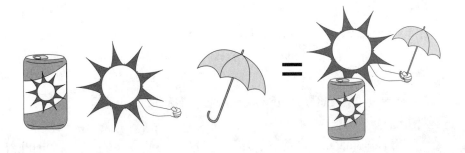

To help lock-in your lesson please play the *Super Memory Transformation* Soundtrack (located on Track #3 of your *Brain Supercharger* CD). Put the book aside for now and make sure to use stereo headphones. Find a comfortable position & quiet place where you can rest undisturbed for the next 30 minutes.

## Step 3: Assessment

You are now ready to test your recall of your special formula represented by the 13-digit number. Mentally run through the link phrase that connects you to the consonants/letters of the Phonetic Code. Then decode those letters into their original numbers. After you are done, compare your numbers to the answer provided and write the total number of correct digits on the score line.

• **Recalling the 13-Digit Number**

— — — — — — — — — — — — —

Your Total Score: _____

(*Answer:* 7280251023945)

Recalling this answer should have been very easy for you if you have followed the previous steps in this workshop. If however, you did not get a perfect score of 13, ask yourself the following questions:

- *Do I know the Phonetic Code?* If not, go back to the previous workshop and review the chart until it becomes automatic.
- *Can I see the link phrase?* If not, repeat Steps 1 and 2 of this workshop.

The Phonetic System is the best memory system for recalling numbers of any length. The more you practice, the easier and quicker you will be able to commit to memory the numbers you use everyday and any new numbers that you come across. The next exercise is a fun and easy way to begin using this system on your own.

## Hit the Road!

License plates offer an ideal training exercise for creating link phrases using the Phonetic Code because on most license plates, half of the information is already letters. Imagine you wanted to remember the license plate AFR-321. To do this, simply use the 3-step process you learned in the preceding workshop:

- Step 1: Transpose the numbers into consonants (refer back to the Phonetic Chart if necessary).
- Step 2: Add the non-numerical letters (a, e, i, o, u, w, h, y, plus silent letters and double letters having the same sounds) to make word phrases.
- Step 3: Link your words into a crazy, illogical, bizarre mental image and lock it in with emotion.

To recall the letters of the license plate, simply use each one as the first letter in a word, which in the given example could be **A** **F**at **R**ed—with the **A** representing itself, the word **F**at representing F and the word **R**ed representing R. Applying the Phonetic Code to 321 could turn the letters MNT, into the word MINT by adding an I. Linking these together would give you A FAT Red MINT.

There are five more license plates below. Use the Phonetic Code and the 3-step process to code the letters and create your own link phrases.

| License Plate | Consonant Code | Link Phrase |
|---|---|---|
| AFR-321 | AFT-MNT | A Fat Red MiNT |
| CPZ-631 | CPZ - _____ | _____ |
| DIW-932 | DIW - _____ | _____ |
| JBO-476 | JBO - _____ | _____ |

FAH-558          FAH - _____          _____

MNR-397          MNR - _____          _____

## Phone Line

For a slightly more challenging exercise, code the following phone numbers into link phrases using the Phonetic Code. Remember that you can chunk the number anyway you wish. There are many possible correct answers for each phone number. The first one is done for you.

| **Phone Number** | **Consonant Code** | **Link Phrase** |
|---|---|---|
| 921-0284 | PNT-SNFR | **PaNTS** oN **FiRe** |
| 322-1929 | _____ | _____ |
| 734-8912 | _____ | _____ |
| 653-0709 | _____ | _____ |
| 222-7839 | _____ | _____ |
| 1-800-479-1532 | _____ | _____ |

## Beyond the Numbers

In the previous two workshops you have learned the final memory system of this course, which has been over 300 years in the making. First developed in 1648, the Phonetic System has undergone many revisions to boost its capabilities while streamlining the rules for the easiest, most powerful system ever.

At first this process might feel slow and very mechanical to you, but so was driving a car, tying your shoe, or using a computer at one time. In a few days this system will begin to flow naturally for you. And when it does, you will be able to memorize long strings of numbers easily—credit cards, insurance ID numbers, social security numbers, phone numbers and more. And this is just the beginning.

In Part III of this book, you'll learn an advanced application of this system which will allow you to recall the order of a deck of 52 cards in random play. But before you advance to this memory feat, there are other advanced applications for you to learn with the Loci and the Peg Systems.

# PART III
# Advanced Memory Applications

# The Peg: Remembering
# Names and Faces

Through the last eight *Photographic Mind Workshops* you have dramatically boosted your ability to record, retain, and retrieve new information. This gift of exceptional memory is something you already had at the beginning of the course, but it was a power that you couldn't tap into because you were never trained in how to use your memory.

Before you move into the Advanced Applications of the systems you've learned, it is important to take the time now to congratulate yourself on the incredible progress you've made throughout this course.

Through the Link, the Loci, the Peg and the Phonetic Systems, you are tapping into the vast territory of your total memory—not just the intellectual memory of your logical left brain and your visual right brain, but the emotional memory of your body as well. In doing so you are expanding your memory powers by 200, 300, 400, and even 500%. It's an exciting process—and a turning point in the lives for those who continue to work with these memory systems to improve their speed and their proficiency in their application.

You now have command of the Link System that will allow you to easily string 20 items together. You also can run through the 20 Loci Props of your Private Retreat to remember another 20 bits of information. You've mastered the Peg System, which not only gives you the ability to store an additional 20 items but lets you directly access them in any sequential order. And lastly, you've expanded your memory even more dramatically with the Phonetic System that allows you to remember numbers of any length.

*You are probably amazed at the leaps and bounds you've made in your ability to remember*. But even more is waiting here for you. In this section of the book you will experience four *Photographic Mind Workshops* that will take you into a higher realm of memory possibilities. It is here that you will <u>fine-tune your</u> <u>newfound skills with specific applications of the Link, Loci, Peg and Phonetic to</u> <u>some of the toughest memory tasks you'll ever face.</u>

## Recalling a Name is as Easy as 1-2-3

You often hear the phrase "I never forget a face." And we simply don't. Why? *Because the mind thinks in pictures.* But, have you ever heard anyone say "Oh, I remember your name but I forget your face?" No—it's the names we forget, not the face. In this workshop you learn that the same power you use to remember the face can just as easily aid you in recalling the name. This is the power of your visual right brain.

In the *Photographic Mind Workshop* titled the Murder Mystery Party you needed to recall the names of all the suspects. However, in that exercise you did not need to match the name to a face.

In real life, however, you do need to match the name to a face. *And names are difficult to recall because they are abstract bits of information—they aren't tangible and can't be pictured.* But, just as you have learned to picture abstract words, such as HEAVEN, you can learn to picture abstract names and hang these pictures onto the person. All you need is the Peg System and a 3-step process.

• **The first step is to turn the name into a picture using word substitution.** In word substitution you have one of two choices: you use a picture that is either a *sound-alike image* or a *symbolic image.* For example, the suspect Senator Maroni was turned into a sound-alike image of macaroni. Macaroni works well because you can see pieces of macaroni and it sounds like Maroni.

An example of a symbolic image would be in the use of an American flag for the name Freely. The flag stands for "freedom," which leads you to the name of Freely. *It's important to remember that the substitute word or symbolic image doesn't need to contain all the exact sounds of the person's name*—as long as you cover the main sound you will have the memory cue you need—and your "true" memory will fill in the rest for you.

• **The second step is to select an outstanding facial feature or article of clothing or jewelry on that person.** This will act as your mental peg. It's best to use the first thing you notice because first impressions are lasting impressions— be it an impression of a big nose, a crazy tie, a beautiful pair of eyes, long sideburns, long dangling earrings or other outstanding features.

You'll notice that there are two types of pegs. <u>There is a permanent peg which is a facial feature of the person. And there is the temporary peg which relates to a "changeable characteristic" such as an article of clothing or jewelry</u>. While the permanent peg, may on the surface, appear to be the better of the two choices, it isn't always. Here's why: while that peg will always be there to remind you of the person's name, the truth is that this type of peg does not give you as many options, nor the most memorable ones either.

A temporary peg such as a scarf, tie, or piece of jewelry, is much easier to peg simply because it is flashy or distinctive. And surprisingly, once you lock that article of clothing or jewelry into memory, this visual image will come back to you the next time you see the person. Your mind is simply quite capable of remembering pictures.

• **The 3rd step is to bring the mental image of the individual's name together with the image of the facial feature or article of clothing/jewelry and connect the two together in a crazy, illogical, bizarre manner.** Use action, exaggeration, and quantity, to vividly visualize your image. And remember to seal in that image with emotion by bringing in all of your senses. The goal is to make an emotional and an intellectual connection with the image you are visualizing.

Using this 3-step process works so well because, in part, it causes you to focus on the person's face. It also forces you to pay attention to the name as it is being introduced to you. And *not paying attention* when an introduction is made is 50% of the problem in forgetting names. Most people are simply absent-minded during introductions, where their mind is focused on themselves (instead of the person being introduced) as they become concerned about *"What am I going to say to this person after we've been introduced?"* or *"Am I going to make a good first impression?"*

Through this 3-step process of matching names to faces you are simply forced to pay attention and really look at the person you are introduced to and listen to hear the name. You cannot peg a facial feature to a name that has been mumbled to you in a rushed introduction. If you haven't heard the name, don't be embarrassed to ask for the name to be repeated. People like to hear their own name. And they will immediately like you because you showed the interest in them by making certain you heard their name correctly.

## Photographic Mind Workshop: Who Dunnit?

## Step 1: Active Learning Session

To enhance your experience of the material please play the *Accelerated Learning Music* soundtrack (located on Track #2 of your *Brain Supercharger* CD) while you complete the following workshop exercise.

Imagine being the sole witness to a drug crime that involved all six suspects from the Murder Mystery Party. The only difference is that this time you do not know their names. To identify the culprits, you have been brought down to Police Headquarters, where a sketch artist is rendering a sketch of each suspect as you describe him or her.

Although you don't know it yet, the Chief of Police has in mind for you a more active role in solving this crime. It seems you have an uncanny likeness to an infamous drug dealer. Although this person has been behind bars for several years, the Chief of Police could easily "leak" to the media that this drug dealer has escaped from prison. Nobody would know that the real drug dealer was still in jail. With you posing as the infamous drug dealer, the Chief of Police could arrange a drug exchange meeting between you and the six culprits and have the evidence he needs to permanently put them behind bars.

He is watching you as you dictate the details to the sketch artist. You definitely look the part with the right build and age. He is impressed with your intelligence and the way you speak. Plus there's a certain moxy about you that would enable you to pull the deal off. Once these suspects are drawn and identified, all you would need to do is memorize their names.

## Reviewing the Artist's Sketches

Look at the sketches and mentally read the words that describe each suspect. As you do, let your right brain focus on the outstanding facial feature or article of clothing/jewelry that you will later use as a mental peg. Let your emotions come into play with the hilarious images you see in your mind to connect you with the name.

Later in this session you'll be asked to verbalize the phrases that mentally hang a person's name with a facial feature or article of clothing/jewelry. The powerful sensory triad of seeing, reading, and verbalizing the material will have you memorizing at an accelerated rate.

### • Suspect #1

The first person you saw was a short balding man—perhaps 5' 4" at the most. The hair he did have was white. He looked to be about 60 years old. He wore wire-rimmed glasses.

### • Suspect #2

The second person you saw was a man with a medium build and dark brown hair. His face was small and round and his eyes were very close together. You don't remember what his nose looked like because your eyes were drawn to his lips. They were unusually large, especially for such a small face. You guess him to be in his early 40s.

### • Suspect #3

The next person is a woman. She was short with medium-length brown hair that was parted on the left and swept behind each ear. You think her eyes were brown and her nose was wide. She had an exceptionally high forehead with deep lines in it—so deep that they may have been scars. Other than the lines on her forehead her skin looked young and she appeared to be in her mid-30's.

### • Suspect #4

Included in this motley group was a distinguished looking man. He was tall—about 6' 2," with sandy gray hair parted on the right. He had steel blue eyes and a pale complexion. He looked to be in his late 50's. He had a long thin nose, and there was a mole on the right side of it. You noticed that the mole moved up when he smiled and then back down again when he relaxed his grin.

### • Suspect #5

The next suspect is a woman. She has chin-length blonde hair and is short, (under 5 ft.) and very skinny. Her eyes were blue-green. She had a ski jump nose. When she smiled you saw she had a huge space between her two front teeth.

• **Suspect #6**

The last suspect is a very tall woman (over 6 ft.) with dark eyes and an olive complexion. She was thin—about 135 pounds. She had long black hair (which was pulled back) and bangs. Two huge earrings dangled from her ears and as she walked they jingled.

## Playing the Part

After the sketches were drawn, an FBI agent was called in to identify the culprits. Based on your accurate descriptions, there was no doubt that the people you saw were the following infamous drug dealers: Dr. Wells, Frank Caswell, Sandy Monarch, Senator Maroni, Betty Lyons and Lisa Berg. Assuming your part in the matter was done, you got up to leave. But as you went to shake the hand of the Chief of Police, he revealed his plan to you for catching the drug dealers and explained the role you would play.

Undecided of what you should do, the Chief of Police assured you of your uncanny likeness to the infamous drug dealer that you would be impersonating. He then showed you a picture of this individual. Indeed, the similarities were striking. You agreed to the deal. The only thing now was to learn the names of the six suspects by tomorrow night—when the drug exchange was to take place. You expressed your concern over learning the names in such a short period of time. At that point, the FBI agent stepped in and offered to show you his foolproof 3-step method:

1. Turn the name into a picture using word substitution.
2. Select an outstanding facial feature or article of clothing or jewelry.
3. Bring together the picture of the name with the facial feature or article of clothing/jewelry together in a crazy, illogical, bizarre manner.

Use the previous cartoon sketches as you go through this 3-step process for the six suspects you described to the sketch artist. After reading through it you will be able to attach not only the following names and faces, but use this same process with other people you meet.

### • Dr. Wells

The first step in this process is to create a vivid mental image of the name through word substitution. At the Murder Mystery Party, you used a water WELL or a wishing WELL to visualize his name. *Which of the two WELLS would produce a better emotional peg—a water well or a wishing well?*

If you said wishing well you are right. A wishing well gives you a strong emotional attachment because it holds the desires that are closest to your heart. A wishing well then, would be an ideal emotional lock to this name. In the first step, you would visualize a WISHING WELL.

The second step is to select a prominent facial peg—either permanent or temporary. In this case you have two ideal permanent pegs—the balding head or the glasses. Let's choose the balding head.

You now have accomplished the first two steps—created a vivid mental image of the individual's name (WISHING WELL) and secondly you have chosen your facial peg (BALDING HEAD).

The third step is to bring these two mental images together—the WISHING WELL and the BALDING HEAD—in a crazy, illogical, bizarre manner that involves action, exaggeration, quantity, uses your senses, evokes emotion and includes you in the picture if possible. And that's easy. You can see yourself throwing pennies into the BALD HEAD as you would a WISHING WELL.

This is a vivid mental picture that is full of emotion for you. But, you're not done yet. You need to add the professional title of Doctor.

Again, you go back to the first step of word substitution. This time, however, you can use a symbolic mental image—that of a STETHOSCOPE. And you can have all the pennies attached to little stethoscopes as you throw them into the well. You now have the entire name Dr. Wells, pegged onto his outstanding facial feature of his bald head.

This took a lot of words to explain these pictures. But visualizing them takes much less time. The mind thinks faster than you can speak or write. And pictures communicate instantly.

### • Frank Caswell

Again, step one is to use the technique of word substitution to create a mental image. In the Murder Mystery Party you used the sound-alike word of CASTLE to form an image for CASWELL. For FRANK you could use a hot dog. That is a symbolic image that is easy to picture. Now, putting these two together in a crazy, illogical, bizarre way you could see a CASTLE made of HOT DOGS.

In step two you need to pick an outstanding facial feature or article of clothing to be your peg. Looking at Frank Caswell, the first thing you notice is his big lips. His big lips then will be your peg.

In step three you mentally hang the castle and hot dogs onto his big lips. You could do this by seeing the lips eating the castle made of hot dogs. This image will lead you to the name of Frank Caswell.

### • Sandy Monarch

You already have an image of a MONARCH BUTTERFLY from the Murder Mystery Party for her last name. And the first name can be simply SAND. Bringing the two together in a crazy manner could give you a mental image of a huge monarch butterfly spreading sand everywhere it flew.

Now take a look at Sandy Monarch. The first thing you notice about her is a high forehead with deep lines in it. By taking the third step in this process you could see that huge monarch butterfly crashing again and again into her forehead spilling sand all over her face. As you do, use your own emotion to empathize with Sandy Monarch and feel the disgust of having sand spilled all over your face.

### • Senator Maroni

I'm sure you remember using MACARONI for Maroni from the Murder Mystery Party. But what can you do for his title—Senator? Using the sound-alike word substitution rule you could use the word CENTER and visualize the center of a circle (represented by a dot inside an oval) or see the Earth cut open to reveal the central core. Either one of these images could be combined with macaroni to give you Senator Maroni.

Now you need to connect it to a facial feature or article of clothing. Looking at the artist's sketch, you are immediately drawn to the mole on the right side of his nose. That's his peg. Hang the macaroni on it. Balance the image of the Earth's central core on it and see fire coming out of the Earth. That mole will light up like a shooting star and there's no way you're ever going to forget his name is Senator Maroni. Just make sure you don't laugh as you say his name!

### • Betty Lyons

In the Murder Mystery Party you used the word LION to remember her last name. And Betty sounds like BED. Visualize a LION throwing a BED. Now, what could the lion be throwing the bed at? Well, let's look at Betty Lyons.

The first thing you notice in the sketch is that huge space between her two front teeth. It looks like a great space for the lion to throw the bed—right between her front teeth. Sounds crazy? It is. Will you remember Betty Lyons? You certainly will.

### • Lisa Berg

The substitute word for her last name at the Murder Mystery Party was iceBERG. For Lisa you can use the MONA LISA. And as you described her to the sketch artist you made special mention of her huge earrings. By visualizing an iceBERG made of EARRINGS ripping through the MONA LISA you can remember the person you're going to meet at the drug heist tomorrow night is of course, Lisa Berg with the big earrings.

## Chunking the Descriptive Peg Phrases

You may be thinking, is matching names to faces really this easy? Yes, it is. And in fact, you can do it much quicker than the time it is taking to read all of this. Again, the mind thinks in pictures and thinks much faster than you can read.

The key to making this system work for you is simply practice. Practice with faces on television, practice with photographs in magazines. Practice with people walking down a busy street. What you're practicing here is picking out prominent facial features or articles of clothing.

To help you match these names with the correct faces, take a moment right now to verbalize the phrases and go through each of the three steps of word substitution, outstanding feature, and pegging the two together.

For Dr. Wells see yourself throwing pennies wearing little STETHOSCOPES into the BALD HEAD as you would a WISHING WELL.

For Frank Caswell see a pair of LIPS eating a CASTLE made of HOT DOGS.

For Sandy Monarch see a huge MONARCH butterfly crashing again and again into her FOREHEAD spilling SAND all over her face.

For Senator Marconi hang a piece of MACARONI on his MOLE and dangling from that macaroni is the Earth's CENtral core, which is spitting out fire.

For Betty Lyons visualize a LION throwing a BED into that SPACE between her FRONT TEETH.

For Lisa Berg visualize an iceBERG made of EARRINGS ripping through the Mona LISA.

## Step 2: Passive Learning Session

The same sketches you saw in the Active Learning Session that bring together a person's name with a prominent feature or article of clothing are shown again on the next page. Spend the next two minutes gazing at them. Try not to concentrate on any one element you see.

As this session is designed for unconscious learning, allowing your mind to wander will give you the maximum benefit. Just relax and let your mind open as you let your eyes move from one image to the next.

To help lock-in your lesson please play the *Super Memory Transformation* Soundtrack (located on Track #3 of your *Brain Supercharger* CD). Put the book aside for now and make sure to use stereo headphones. Find a comfortable position & quiet place where you can rest undisturbed for the next 30 minutes.

## Step 3: Assessment

The drug heist is about to come down. You are at the agreed upon location and time, waiting for the six drug dealers to make their entrance. All you need to do is convince them of your identity and then make the exchange. The FBI agents are stationed at strategic points to secure your safety and rush in to arrest the six suspects.

You rehearse their names in your mind as you mentally match each name to a face. You know the drug dealers are suspicious. One slip-up from you could spell disaster. But you can't think of that now. Suddenly you see one of them, then two, then three, then all six. They address you by the name of the individual you are impersonating and ask for you to identify them. Suddenly you feel braver than you are. Without a sign of the terror you feel you casually call out their names.

Write the name below each picture. Then show how you arrived at each name by writing the answers in the chart on the next page. When you are done, compare your list to the answers provided and write your total number of correct answers on the score line (each correct answer is worth one point).

1.  2.  3.  4.  5.  6.

_____   _____   _____   _____   _____   _____

| Person | Substitute Word | Substitute Word | Pegging Feature |
|---|---|---|---|
| Dr. Wells | _____ | _____ | _____ |
| Frank Caswell | _____ | _____ | _____ |
| Sandy Monarch | _____ | _____ | _____ |
| Senator Maroni | _____ | _____ | _____ |
| Betty Lyons | _____ | _____ | _____ |
| Lisa Berg | _____ | _____ | _____ |

Your Total Score: _____

*(Answers: Dr. Wells—stethoscopes, wishing well, bald head; Frank Caswell—hot dog, castle, lips; Sandy Monarch—sand, butterfly, forehead; Senator Maroni—Earth's central core, macaroni, mole; Betty Lyons—bed, lion, space between front teeth; Lisa Berg—Mona Lisa, iceberg, earrings)*

Did you get all the names right and fill in the chart correctly? If you got 21 or more correct, you are ready to try the 3-step process on your own. No two faces are alike. And the more you practice looking at them, the more categories of specific facial features you will begin to notice. What you need to do is build some internal maps of facial features. The next section will give you helpful hints on how to do this. Then, you can apply this information immediately to a sample of eight faces that follow the section.

## Creating Memory Maps of Facial Features

While at first it may seem easier to use articles of clothing or jewelry as pegs, the permanent facial features offer many different characteristics as well. The more you know what to look for, the more these differences will leap out at you. In this section you'll get some helpful hints for categorizing noses, eyes, chins, foreheads and more so that you can easily use them as pegs.

### • Hair

As you look at a face, ask yourself the following: Is the hair thick, fine, receding, or bald? Look at the part—is it way down on the side or straight as an arrow down the middle. What about the lines of the hair—wavy, kinky curls, or straight? Now look at the cut—crew cut, buzz cut, Dutch Boy style with bangs and straight sides, angel-look with wings off the face, or the baseball-look with a bun sitting on top of the head? And don't forget color, plus the degree of gray—salt and pepper, silver gray, or white as the snow.

### • Shape of the Face

Now look at the overall shape of the head. Fat head, pin head, or medium size? How about the shape of the face? Some are like hearts (or triangles), others are round with full cheeks, some long and think, or a basic square.

Focus also on the forehead. It is high or low? Is it full of lines or smooth and taut? Some foreheads are extremely wide. Others seem almost too thin for the shape of the face. Do you see a widow's peak?

### • Eyebrow and Eyes

Are the eyebrows long? Short? Bushy? Are they thin and very sparse? What is their shape—flat, winged, arched or tapered? And finally, how close together are the eyebrows—do they meet in the middle or stay on their separate sides?

Now for the eyes. The eyes are the windows to the soul. And they truly are one of the most distinctive facial features. When you look at the eyes, first notice the eyelashes—are they long and thick, short and stubby, straight or curly? Notice the color of the lashes too—are they same as the eyebrows or different? Are they tilted up or down?

Also, look at the slant of the eyes. Tilted up or down? Look at their shape—almond, very round yet flat, or full and bulgy. Maybe they are beady—meaning small and narrow—or shifty with the pupils darting here and there. Does the person stare at you or gaze at you? Do the eyes crinkle when the person smiles?

Of course you'll notice the color of the eyes immediately. But don't just think blue—think gray blue, hazel blue, ice blue, blue green. And green eyes range from brownish green to aquamarine green to almost a yellow cat's eye.

What about the space between the eyes—are the eyes close together or spaced far apart? Something you might miss is how the iris (the colored part of the eye) sits in the socket. Some eyes seem to float slightly above the bottom eyelid, others rest centered. And what about the eyelids—thin and light, or heavy and hanging? Look under the eyes for extra baggage too.

### • Nose

Now let's go on to the nose. First, look at the overall size—small, medium, or a real honker. Is it long or short? Is it straight, pug, or does it lightly lift up? Is there a bump on it, or a mole, or freckles? Some noses are wide and flat, others are very thin and delicate. And finally, are the nostrils hairy?

### • Cheek Bones

Next, check out the cheek bones. Some people don't seem to have any—their face seems pushed in. Others have cheek bones riding high up into their eyes. Some cheeks are drawn, while others are so full and round you just want to pinch them.

### • Ears

What peg can be better than the ears! Big? Small? Or normal size? Look at the lobes—huge and chunky or slight and skimpy. What about the shape of the ear—round or oblong? And do they protrude out or do they lie flat against the head?

### • Lips, Smiles, and Teeth

Are the lips big, small, or just the right size? Are they full or thick—or is one different from the other? Does one protrude more than the other? Do you notice any scars or bumps? Does one or both sides turn up or down?

And look at the smile. Is it wide, expansive and sincere? Or do the lips barely turn up? When the person smiles can you see their teeth? And if so, are the teeth crooked, straight, chipped, white or discolored, or is there a space between them as with our suspect Betty Lyons?

Some people smile so much you see their top and bottom teeth. Some people smile and their dimples jump out at you. Sometimes a person's mouth looks like a horse's mouth and others like a beaver. Think to yourself "why" behind these cliches and you'll begin to build these maps of facial features into your memory.

### • Chin

Also look at the chin. Some stick out, others seem to get lost in the skin. Then you need to count them—one chin, double chin, triple chin, or more. Is there a cleft in the chin? Is it a square chin, pointed chin, or round?

### • Skin

The color and texture of the skin is another area to notice. Is it dark, light, blemished or clear? Some skin appears rough, other skin looks smooth. It also can be oily, dry, or wrinkled. Be aware of moles and scars as well.

Although this may seem like an enormous amount of specific facial characteristics, you can easily come up with even more on your own. All you need to do is practice looking at people—really studying their faces as they talk and smile. The best place to begin this activity is with the following pages in this book.

## Guess Who?

This exercise gives you the opportunity to use the 3-step process you learned in this *Photographic Mind Workshop* to remember the name of each person pictured on the next page. Here's how:

1. Create a vivid mental image of the name (a picture word) through word substitution using sound-alike words or symbolic words.
2. Choose either a permanent peg (facial feature) or a temporary peg (article of clothing or jewelry).
3. Connect the two together in a crazy, illogical, bizarre way and lock that image in with emotion.

**Marsha Hartung**

Word Substitution: _____

Peg: _____

Mental Image: _____

**Richard Rockford**

Word Substitution: _____

Peg: _____

Mental Image: _____

**Craig Polinski**

Word Substitution: _____

Peg: _____

Mental Image: _____

**Rose Lambert**

Word Substitution: _____

Peg: _____

Mental Image: _____

**Dr. Wayne Steinfield**

Word Substitution: _____

Peg: _____

Mental Image: _____

**Mary Hutchinson**

Word Substitution: _____

Peg: _____

Mental Image: _____

**Thomas Falconi**

Word Substitution: _____

Peg: _____

Mental Image: _____

**Elaine Livingston**

Word Substitution: _____

Peg: _____

Mental Image: _____

When you have completed this exercise, close the book and take a 10 minute break. Then come back to this section of the book and test yourself with the following quiz entitled "Photo Finish."

## It's a Photo Finish!

Without looking at the previous exercise, identify the 8 people you see here.

## Creating Memory Maps of Names and Titles

The first time you come across a name, for example the name Betty, you need to create a word substitution and then visualize the image. But thereafter, you can use the same word substitution and visual icon for every Betty you meet. They all have different last names, so you will never be confused between the two Bettys.

The advantage of this process is that you can link the name faster because half of it—the first name—is already done for you. These "standard" icons allow you to meet 5 or 6 people in rapid succession and remember each person's name.

The first Bonus Memory Map at the end of this chapter gives you a head start on meeting almost 300 people. On these pages you can build your own vocabulary of instant picture-name pegs for 300 commonly found names. By doing this you're creating a memory map of names, and are likely to have half of the person's name already into a visual icon the first time you meet him or her.

Next to each name there is ample room to write your picture-word for it. Remember to use the word substitution techniques of sound-alike or symbolic images. Do not feel compelled to finish this exercise in one sitting. Instead, break it down into chunks of 10 names and do a chunk or two a day. By the time you are done, you will find that the pictures come back easily to you. Again, the mind remembers what it creates.

This book also contains a second Bonus Memory Map for titles, such as President and Vice President. There is also room for you to fill in some of the major companies you need to know in your professional life. Company names can be added on in a similar manner to titles.

To keep things clear in your mind (as to which picture is representing what element—either title, first name, last name or company name) you need to "stack" or "grow" your pictures in a consistent order—just as you moved in a consistent fashion around your Loci.

For example, imagine the name you wanted to remember was Bill Marston, President of Singerbrook, and the facial feature you wanted to hang all this on was a beard. Your could use a duckBILL for his first name, and a MARTIAN for his second name. This would result in a visual icon of a Martian peering into a bill of a duck, who is of course wearing a beard.

The next step is to put the name of the company under this image, as follows: The duck is standing in a BROOK made out of the musical notes which are SINGING (you can see their mouths open and close). Then put the title above the first name/last name picture. On top of the duckbill and Martian the WHITE HOUSE (for President) was tumbling, as in an earthquake.

The order here in this stack of names is the title on top, the first name/last name in the middle, and the company name on the bottom. By always following this order you will know which picture is referring to which part of the name.

Let's look at a few more titles. If the WHITE HOUSE stands for President, what could Vice President be? How about a giant Vice crushing the WHITE HOUSE? That would work. And what about the title Professor? That one could be a symbolic image of a BOOK. The beauty in this system is that you can think of a picture for every name, company name or business title. All it takes is a little imagination and practice.

## Bonus Memory Map: Icons for 300 Common Names

| Female Names | Your Icon |
| --- | --- |
| Abby | a bee |
| Abigail | |
| Ada | |
| Adelle | |
| Adora | |
| Adrian | |
| Agatha | |
| Agnes | |
| Aileen | |
| Alberta | |
| Alexandra | |
| Alexis | |
| Alice | |
| Alison | |
| Alixe | |
| Alyssa | |
| Amanda | |
| Ambrose | |
| Amelia | |
| Amy | |
| Andrea | |
| Angela | |

Angelica

Angie

Anita

Ann

Anna

Annette

Antoinette

April

Arlene

Audrey

Ava

Barbara

Becky

Belinda

Bernadette

Bernadine

Bernice

Beth

Betty

Bev

Beverly

Bobbi

Brenda

Bridget

Camille

Candace

Carla

Carlotta

Carol

Catherine

Ceal

Cecillia

Charlene

Charlotte

Charmaine

Chris

Christina

Cindy

Claire

Claudia

Colleen

Connie

Cynthia

Daisy

Darlene

Dawn

Debbie

Denise

Desiree

Diane

Diana

Dina

Dolores

Donna

Doris

Dorothy

Dottie

Edith

Edna

Eileen

Elaine

Eleanor

Elena

Elizabeth

Ellen

Erica

Eva

Evelyn

Faith

Flora

Frances

Georgia

Ginny

Gloria

Grace

Harriett

Heather

Helen

Helena

Hope

Ida

Irene

Jacqueline

Jane

Janet

Jean

Jennifer

Jessica

Jill

Joan

Joanna

Jocelyn

Josephine

Joy

Joyce

Juanita

Judy

Julia

Julie

Juliet

June

Justine

Kara

Karen

Kate

Kathleen

Kathy

Kay

Kitty

Krista

Kristin

Laura

Leslie

Lillian

Linda

Lisa

Lois

Lora

Lorrain

Lucy

Luisa

Lynn

Madonna

Maggie

Marcie

Margaret

Marge

Margy

Maria _____

Marian _____

Marilyn _____

Marsha _____

Mary _____

Maureen _____

Maxine _____

Melanie _____

Melissa _____

Michelle _____

Millie _____

Mimi _____

Molly _____

Nancy _____

Natalie _____

Nelly _____

Netta _____

Nina _____

Nita _____

Nora _____

Pam _____

Pat _____

Patricia _____

Patty _____

Paula _____

Pauline _____

Peg _____

Peggy _____

Phyllis _____

Polly _____

Rachel _____

Regina _____

Rita

Roberta

Ronnie

Rosa

Rosalie

Rose

Rosemary

Rosie

Ruth

Sally

Sandra

Sandy

Sara

Sharon

Sheila

Silvia

Sonia

Stella

Stephanie

Sue

Susan

Susanna

Suzie

Terri

Theresa

Tina

Toni

Valerie

Vanessa

Vera

Veronica

Vicky

Victoria _____

Virginia _____

Wanda _____

Wendy _____

Yvonne _____


**Male Names**                          **Your Icon**

Aaron _____

Abott _____

Abdul _____

Adam _____

Al _____

Alan _____

Albert _____

Alec _____

Alex _____

Alexander _____

Alfred _____

Alphonse _____

Andrew _____

Andy _____

Anthony _____

Arnold _____

Art _____

Artie _____

Barry _____

Ben _____

Bill _____

Billy _____

Bob _____

Bobby _____

Brandan _____

Brian

Bruce

Bud

Buddy

Burt

Carl

Chad

Charles

Chris

Christopher

Chuck

Clark

Colin

Dan

Daniel

Danny

Dave

David

Dennis

Dominic

Don

Donald

Doug

Ed

Eric

Eugene

Fran

Francis

Frank

Franny

Fred

Gavin

Gene

George

Gerald

Greg

Gregory

Hank

Harold

Harry

Henry

Jack

Jacob

James

Jamie

Jared

Jason

Jeff

Jeffrey

Jerry

Jim

Joseph

John

Justin

Ken

Kenneth

Kevin

Keith

Larry

Leo

Linus

Lou

Luke

Mark

Martin

Matt

Matthew

Max

Michael

Mike

Nathan

Nicholas

Nick

Oscar

Pat

Patrick

Paul

Pete

Peter

Phil

Philip

Quincy

Ralph

Randy

Ray

Raymond

Rich

Richard

Rick

Rob

Robert

Roger

Ron

Ronald

Roy

Salvatore

Sam

Sean

Sidney

Silvester

Simon

Stan

Stanley

Stephen

Steve

Ted

Teddy

Theo

Theodore

Thomas

Tim

Timmy

Timothy

Toby

Tom

Tommy

Tony

Vance

Vick

Victor

Walt

Walter

Will

William

Willy

Zachary

# Bonus Memory Map: Icons for Professional Titles and Company Names

| Titles | Your Icon |
|---|---|
| President | |
| Vice President | |
| Director | |
| Manager | |
| Doctor | |
| Professor | |
| Other Titles | |
| | |
| | |
| | |

| Company Names | Your Icon |
|---|---|
| | |
| | |
| | |
| | |
| | |
| | |
| | |
| | |
| | |

# The Loci: Reciting Winning Speeches & Presentations

In the previous *Photographic Mind Workshop* you applied the Peg System to the challenging task of remembering names and faces. In the upcoming workshop you will advance to a more difficult memory task of giving winning speeches and sales presentations with the utmost of ease—and without the use of note cards. To do so you will use the Loci System.

Before you begin, refresh your memory by reviewing the 20 Loci props of your Private Retreat. In the first room, the living room, the first five props are the:

- grand piano
- Queen Anne chair
- marble fireplace
- oriental rug
- cherry wood desk

In room two, the kitchen, the next five props are the:

- espresso machine
- green-tiled cooking island
- walk-in pantry
- oak table
- mirrored refrigerator

In room three, the entertainment room, the next five props are the:

- grandfather clock
- wet bar
- seven foot television screen
- black leather couch
- built-in bookcase

And in the final room, the tropical sun room, the last five props are the:

• sea grass hammock
• saltwater aquarium
• river rock waterfall
• gilded bird cage
• bubbling hot springs

## Using Your Loci Props as Cue Cards

To use the Loci System to remember a speech, you hang key words of the main ideas in your speech onto each prop in your Private Retreat. Then, as you give your speech, you imagine your loci props as they appear in a sequential order. Each prop reminds you of the key word you pegged to it, and each word will remind you of what you want to say next.

In this way, your speech will follow the logical order in which it was written. And yet you'll be able to deliver this logically ordered speech without the use of any note cards whatsoever—and without having to memorize it word for word.

This ability to give a speech without memorizing it will turn you into an exceptional speaker because it will allow you to deliver the speech in a natural tone of voice. Plus, because the props are from the comfortable setting of your Private Retreat, you are automatically put into a relaxed state as you make your speech.

Your spontaneous and energetic performance will draw your audience in and engage their attention with a command you have never known before. Suddenly, you will no longer dread giving speeches. In fact, you will love giving speeches, because everyone loves to do what they excel at. And using the Loci System to give a speech will enable you to excel at public presentations of any kind.

The upcoming *Photographic Mind Workshop* takes you to an art museum, where you have volunteered to become a tour guide. Before you can lead your first tour group, you need to memorize a short speech introducing your guests to the world of art and to some of the individual pieces of art found in your museum.

# Photographic Mind Workshop: Becoming a Tour Guide

## Step 1: Active Learning Session

**To enhance your experience of the material please play the *Accelerated Learning Music* soundtrack (located on Track #2 of your *Brain Supercharger* CD) while you complete the following workshop exercise.**

To prepare you for your first day as a tour guide in the art museum, the Docent Director has given you a speech to memorize. The purpose of the speech is to give a brief introduction to art in general, and highlight certain works of art in the museum's collection.

The speech is printed in this book for you to read. Please pay specific attention to the boldface words, as these are the key words, or the main ideas, of the speech that will be hung on your 20 loci props.

A little further into the session you'll be shown step-by-step how to hang the boldface key words onto each prop in your Private Retreat. This will allow your brain to connect with the flow of the speech as it takes a mental caravan through your Private Retreat.

Finally, you'll verbalize the speech out loud, reading it word for word from the book.

## The Language of Art

*The art contained in this museum comes from all over **the world**. The artists come from different countries and speak different languages. Yet we **don't need to speak** their language to understand their art. That is the beauty of art. It speaks to us, it communicates to us in a language all its own. It's a language we can all understand. It is a language of **color, shape, and line**.*

*The **primary colors** are red, yellow, and blue. Some basic **shapes** are a square, a circle, a rectangle, and a triangle. And lines connect it all.*

*A line is nothing more than a **series of dots** bunched closely together all in a* *row. A line is said to have a derivation and a destination—it is coming from somewhere and it is going somewhere. By **stacking lines** on top of each other you form a solid block—just as the action of closing the blinds on a window creates a solid to block out the light. This block is called a **plane**. And it is indeed a shape. Art is a language of **shape, line, and color**. And it speaks to us all.*

*As you **look** at the beautiful pieces of artwork in these rooms and on these walls, involve yourself by involving your senses. **Trace** the lines of a painting in the air with your own hand. **Identify** the different colors used to paint a single leaf. See the sculptured **wolf** and hear his lone cry echo down the mountain. Observe the oil painting of **strawberries** covered in whipped cream and taste their sweetness. And as you come upon the watercolor of the **rose garden**, walk through that garden in your mind's eye and take in the sweet-smelling scent that fills the air.*

*Use all your **senses** to take in the art here. And know that as you do this, you are being an **artist too**. For being an artist is something you already know—being an artist is **observing** the world around you. It's a world **captured** by the artists of many countries who all use the language of color, shape, and line to communicate their feelings for all time, and for all people. I **invite** you to share it all here on your visit today.*

If you felt yourself panicking at the thought of memorizing this speech, that's okay. Don't worry, this is normal! Because the scope of the speech is unfamiliar to you, there are many more key words in this speech than you would normally have in just a few paragraphs.

Obviously, when you give a speech that you have written, you are familiar with the subject knowledge—*remembering what* you want to say about each thought is not the problem—*knowing the order and perhaps forgetting to cover a topic* is the problem. And that's how the Loci System can save you—by giving you an order for your key points.

## How to Hang Key Ideas on Your Loci Props

The speech is printed below again for you. Only this time it contains icons to be used as visual mental images. Each of these icons represents a boldface phrase as hung onto one of the 20 loci props of your Private Retreat.

As you mentally read the speech, focus on the icon and let it reconnect you with your Loci prop. Below each line is a step-by-step description of how the icon is hung onto your loci prop.

SPEECH: The art contained in this museum comes from all over **the world**. The artists come from different countries and speak different languages.
IMAGE: *Hang a mental image of the "world" blowing up on your piano.*

SPEECH: Yet we **don't need to speak** their language to understand their art. That is the beauty of art. It speaks to us, it communicates to us in a language all its own.
IMAGE: *See a lock hanging on your lips (for "don't speak") and see yourself kissing the Queen Ann chair.*

SPEECH: It's a language we can all understand. It is a language of **color, shape, and line**.
IMAGE: *Using a crayon (for color), the dotted outline of a murdered victim (for shape), and a clothes line (for line), combine them together to create a visual image of a murdered victim's shape hanging from the clothes line and dripping red colored crayons onto the marble fireplace.*

SPEECH: The **primary colors** are red, yellow, and blue.

IMAGE: *Hang a mental image of "primary colors" by seeing gigantic red, yellow and blue crayons coloring all over the oriental rug.*

SPEECH: Some basic **shapes** are a square, a circle, a rectangle, and a triangle. And lines connect it all.

IMAGE: *Hang a mental image of "shapes" by seeing cookie cutter shapes cutting the cherry wood desk to pieces.*

SPEECH: A line is nothing more than a **series of dots** bunched closely together all in a row. A line is said to have a derivation and a destination—it is coming from somewhere and it is going somewhere.

IMAGE: *Hang a mental image of the "series of dots" by seeing dots of coffee beans jumping all over the espresso machine.*

SPEECH: By **stacking lines** on top of each other you form a solid block—just as the action of closing the blinds on a window creates a solid to block out the light.

IMAGE: *Hang a mental image of lines of people stacked on top of each other, passing the cooking island from the front of the line to the back.*

SPEECH: This block is called a **plane**. And it is indeed a shape.

IMAGE: *Hang the mental image of "plane" by visualizing your pantry flying on top of a plane.*

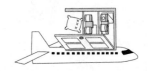

SPEECH: Art is a language of **shape, line, and color**. And it speaks to us all.

IMAGE: *Hang the mental image of the murdered victim's outline swinging from the clothes line, dripping red crayons on the oak table. Now the order of the 3 words here—shape, line and color—is different in this instance from the first time in your speech—but your true memory will fill that in.*

SPEECH: As you **look** at the beautiful pieces of artwork in these rooms and on these walls, involve yourself by involving your senses.

IMAGE: *Hang the mental image of an "eye" (for look) by visualizing your eyes all over the mirrors on the refrigerator.*

SPEECH: **Trace** the lines of a painting in the air with your own hand.

IMAGE: *Hang the mental image of a "stencil" (for trace) over the face of the grandfather clock.*

SPEECH: **Identify** the different colors used to paint a single leaf.

IMAGE: *Hang the mental image of "many pointed fingers" (for identify) on the wet bar by seeing fingers in all the cocktail glasses.*

SPEECH: See the sculptured **wolf** and hear his lone cry echo down the mountain.

IMAGE: *Hang the mental image of a gigantic "wolf" staring at you on the seven foot television screen.*

SPEECH: Observe the oil painting of **strawberries** covered in whipped cream and taste their sweetness.

IMAGE: *Hang the mental image of "strawberries" covering your body as you lay on the black leather couch.*

SPEECH: And as you come upon the watercolor of the **rose garden**, walk through that garden in your mind's eye and take in the sweet-smelling scent that fills the air.

IMAGE: *Hang the mental image of the "rose garden" by seeing rows of roses sprouting from the books on the built-in bookcase.*

SPEECH: Use all your **senses** to take in the art here.

IMAGE: *Hang the mental image of "pennies" (for cents, sounds like senses) dropping all over you as you relax on the sea grass hammock.*

SPEECH: And know that as you do this, you are being an **artist too**.

IMAGE: *Hang the mental image of "artist too" by seeing two artist berets (symbolic for artist too) floating in the saltwater aquarium.*

SPEECH: For being an artist is something you already know—being an artist is **observing** the world around you.

IMAGE: *Hang the mental image of "observing" by seeing the river rock waterfall come pouring through the lenses of a pair of binoculars.*

SPEECH: It's a world **captured** by the artists of many countries who all use the language of color, shape, and line to communicate their feelings for all time, and for all people.

IMAGE: *Hang a mental image of a "butterfly in a net" (for captured) being eaten by the pair of cockatoos in the gilded cage.*

SPEECH: I **invite** you to share it all here on your visit today.

IMAGE: *Hang a mental image of hundreds of "wedding invitations" (for invite) floating around you as you relax in the bubbling hot springs.*

Are the major points in the speech becoming easier to recall? They should be. Yet, if you weren't able to jump ahead to the next point before hearing it, don't be discouraged. This speech is reprinted below again for you. Yet now, it uses the icon as a prompt next to the corresponding line in the speech.

This time, verbalize the speech out loud and focus only on the icons to help you recall the words. If you aren't able to recite it completely from memory, the words are printed there for you.

SPEECH: The art contained in this museum comes from all over **the world**. The artists come from different countries and speak different languages.

SPEECH: Yet we **don't need to speak** their language to understand their art. That is the beauty of art. It speaks to us, it communicates to us in a language all its own.

SPEECH: It's a language we can all understand. It is a language of **color, shape, and line**.

SPEECH: The **primary colors** are red, yellow, and blue.

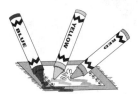

SPEECH: Some basic **shapes** are a square, a circle, a rectangle, and a triangle. And lines connect it all.

SPEECH: A line is nothing more than a **series of dots** bunched closely together all in a row. A line is said to have a derivation and a destination— it is coming from somewhere and it is going somewhere.

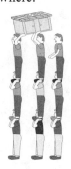

SPEECH: By **stacking lines** on top of each other you form a solid block—just as the action of closing the blinds on a window creates a solid to block out the light.

SPEECH: This block is called a **plane**. And it is indeed a shape.

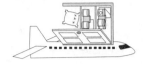

SPEECH: Art is a language of **shape, line, and color**. And it speaks to us all.

SPEECH: As you **look** at the beautiful pieces of artwork in these rooms and on these walls, involve yourself by involving your senses.

SPEECH: **Trace** the lines of a painting in the air with your own hand.

SPEECH: **Identify** the different colors used to paint a single leaf.

SPEECH: See the sculptured **wolf** and hear his lone cry echo down the mountain.

SPEECH: Observe the oil painting of **strawberries** covered in whipped cream and taste their sweetness.

SPEECH: And as you come upon the watercolor of the **rose garden**, walk through that garden in your mind's eye and take in the sweet-smelling scent that fills the air.

SPEECH: Use all your **senses** to take in the art here.

SPEECH: And know that as you do this, you are being an **artist too**.

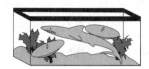

SPEECH: For being an artist is something you already know—being an artist is **observing** the world around you.

SPEECH: It's a world **captured** by the artists of many countries who all use the language of color, shape, and line to communicate their feelings for all time, and for all people.

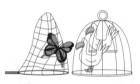

SPEECH: I **invite** you to share it all here on your visit today.

## Step 2: Passive Learning Session

The icons from the speech you saw in the Active Learning Session that represent the main ideas of the speech are shown again below. Spend the next two minutes gazing at them. Try not to concentrate on any one icon that you see.

As this session is designed for unconscious learning, allowing your mind to wander will give you the maximum benefit. Just relax and let your mind open as you sweep through the whole speech in an easy and flowing motion.

To help lock-in your lesson please play the *Super Memory Transformation* Soundtrack (located on Track #3 of your *Brain Supercharger* CD). Put the book aside for now and make sure to use stereo headphones. Find a comfortable position & quiet place where you can rest undisturbed for the next 30 minutes.

## Step 3: Assessment

Your first tour at the art museum is now gathering in the reception area. You put on your Docent Badge, take a deep breath and walk out to meet your guests with a welcoming smile on your face.

You feel confident. You feel accomplished. You feel prepared. As well you should! For you are after all, about to walk these people through an art museum and a presentation that is very much a part of you because it takes place in your own Private Retreat. You know this place inside and out, and are very comfortable in these beautiful surroundings.

To see how well you are able to present the speech without the use of any notes, take the final test below. Here you'll see the twenty key points of the speech, all in a random order. Your challenge is to number them 1 through 20 in the order as each would appear in the speech.

To do this, simply take a mental caravan of your Private Retreat (starting with the grand piano) and number the order in which you see each of the following key phrases pop into your head. When you are done, compare your list to the answers provided and write your total number of correct answers on the score line (each correct answer is worth one point).

## Recalling the Order of the Main Parts in Your Speech

__ wolf
__ the world
__ plane

__ artist too

__ primary colors

__ captured by

__ series of dots

__ don't need to speak

__ rose garden

__ shapes

__ strawberries

__ look

__ senses

__ trace

__ observing

__ color, shape, and line

__ shape, line, and color

__ invite

__ stacking lines

__ identify

Your Total Score: _____

(Answers: *wolf* is #13, *the world* is #1, *plane* is #8, *artist too* is #17, *primary colors* is #4, *captured by* is #19, *series of dots* is #6, *don't need to speak* is #2, *rose garden* is #15, *strawberries* is #5, *shapes* is #14, *look* is #10, *senses* is #16, *trace* is #11, *observing* is #18, *color, shape and line* is #3, *shape, line and color* is #20, *invite* is #9, *stacking lines* is #7 and *identify* is #12)

If your score was 18 or more, you're doing great. Yet many people who are able to put the key phrases in the correct order still feel they aren't comfortable with reciting the speech. The reason for this is because, until this exercise, you probably knew little about the subject of art.

If you were a real tour guide, you would be familiar with the subject of art and the exhibits at the museum. You would know, for instance, that the wolf was a sculpture, the strawberries were an oil painting, and the rose garden was a watercolor. The fact that you are able to remember the key points in this speech, and to recall them in their proper order, demonstrates the power of the Loci System.

## Practice on a Speech of Your Own

Before continuing on with this book, take the knowledge you've gained in this *Photographic Mind Workshop* and apply it to a speech or presentation that you wrote yourself by:

> 1. Turning major points of the material into key words.
> 2. Hanging those key words on the loci props of your Private Retreat.

Again, the mind does not forget what it creates. You will be amazed at how easy it is to recall the material. This in turn will give the confidence you need to turn your presentation into a winning performance!

After you feel confident in your ability to use the advanced memory application of the Loci System presented in this section, you are ready to progress into the final two *Photographic Mind Workshops*. Here you will unleash your memory powers by combining the strengths of the Link, the Loci, and the Peg System. In this final display of your photographic mind you will perform the incredible memory feat of naming the one missing card from a deck of 52 randomly played cards.

# The Phonetic: Recalling a Deck of 52 Cards

In the previous two workshops you've learned how to recall names and give winning speeches and presentations with advanced memory applications of the Peg and Loci Systems. In this final workshop you'll learn how to win at the card table with an advanced memory application of the Phonetic System and the Link System combined.

This lesson is an especially intriguing one for most people—especially if you have dreams of winning it big in Las Vegas. Even if you play an occasional game of cards, you will improve your chances of winning considerably by applying the techniques you'll learn here. While winning at cards does involve a little luck, it also requires well-honed skills—the skills for playing your cards well and the skills for playing your memory well. With the use of the Phonetic System and the Link System you can remember not only an entire deck of cards, but the order in which each was played!

## Visualizing the Cards

To most people, cards are hard to remember because they are intangible, they are abstracts. Yet the way to make these abstracts more memorable is to convert them into something that can be pictured through word substitution. Once you form a picture-word, you can lock it into memory with emotion.

The challenge then is to picture each of the 52 cards in the deck. And you can do this by applying the Phonetic Code with a new twist. That twist is an easy one—each of the picture-words (representing the 52 cards) will begin with the letter of the suit name. Therefore C is Clubs, D is Diamonds, H is Hearts, and S is Spades.

Next, you need to apply the Phonetic Code to make a picture-word. It's easy when you follow this first ground rule:

*The consonant sound following the beginning letter will be the Number Code that represents the value of the card.*

For example, take the 2 of Diamonds. Diamonds begins with a D therefore, the picture-word you are creating to represent the 2 of Diamonds must begin with a D. The consonant sound for 2 is two strokes down for N. So the 2 of diamonds translates into DN. Now you just add non-numerical letters (which are the vowels and the letters in the word WHY) to form a word. We'll add a U after the D and an E after the N to form the word DUNE. DUNE is the picture-word for the 2 of Diamonds.

Let's try another card. What could be a picture-word for the 8 of Hearts? It will begin with H, and have either an F or V in it (for the number 8). Let's choose the F. By adding the non-numerical vowels OO in between H and F you get HOOF. HOOF is then the picture-word for the 8 of Hearts.

## 6 Ground Rules for Creating Picture-Words

The upcoming workshop will show you step-by-step how to commit these 52 picture-words to memory. And to make it even easier, here are some ground rules to follow. You already know the first two, but they are repeated here again for you.

- Each of the picture-words begin with the letter of the suit name.
- The consonant sound following the beginning letter is the Number Code that represents the value of the card.
- Aces have a value of 1 which tells you the picture-word for an ace has either the letter T or D in it (the Phonetic Code for 1 is represented by a T or D).
- The 10 is counted as a 0 rather than combining the two digits of 1 plus 0. (There is no 0 in a deck of cards, so using the 0 for the 10 does not represent a problem.)

- The picture-word for the King is simply the suit's namesake—either a Club, Heart, Spade or Diamond. Therefore, the King of Diamonds is just a Diamond, the King of Spades is just a Spade, and so on.
- The Jack is counted as an 11 (which is represented by two "T"s or 2 "D"s or one of each. And the Queen is counted as a 12 (represented by a T or D followed by an N).

With these rules and the knowledge of the Phonetic Code, you can see every card as a picture-word and remember every card that is played on the table. The following workshop will take you through this process step-by-step.

## Photographic Mind Workshop: 52 Card Recall

### Step 1: Active Learning Session

**To enhance your experience of the material please play the** *Accelerated Learning Music* **soundtrack (located on Track #2 of your** *Brain Supercharger* **CD) while you complete the following workshop exercise.**

During this step you will follow along in your workbook as you learn the picture-words created from the Phonetic Code for each of the 13 cards in the suits of Clubs, Diamonds, Hearts and Spades.

The emphasis here is on <u>learning</u>, not <u>memorizing</u>. Each picture-word is created from the Phonetic Code, which is based upon the associations with the letter/consonant sounds and the digits 0 through 9, plus the number value of the card. You already know these associations. You just need to reconnect with them through a new map in your mind that organizes the information in a way that is useful to you.

As you see each word, mentally run through the Phonetic Code along with the 6 guidelines for making picture-cards to understand the reason for that word. A little further into the session you'll verbalize the picture-words out loud as you mentally turn over the playing cards. Let's begin with the suit of Clubs.

• **The Ace of Clubs is CAT.**

Now, ask yourself "Why CAT?" By using the 6 rules from above you can quickly understand why: The suit of Clubs begins with a "C," the Phonetic Code for 1 (representing the ace) is "T," and the fill-in letter (with no numerical value) is the vowel "A."

• **The 2 of Clubs is CAN.**

Again, ask yourself "Why CAN?" Club begins with a "C," the code for 2 is "N," and the fill-in letter (with no numerical value) is again the vowel "A." If you know your Phonetic Code you also know that the letter in the position of the "A" could be any vowel, or the letters "WHY" or any silent letter.

• **The 3 of Clubs is COMB.**

Again, ask yourself "Why COMB?" Club begins with a "C," the code for 3 is "M," and the fill-in letters (with no numerical value) are the vowel "O" and the silent letter "B."

• **The 4 of Clubs is CAR.**

Again, ask yourself "Why CAR?" Club begins with "C," the code for 4 is "R" and the fill-in letter is the vowel "A."

• **The 5 of Clubs is COAL.**

Again, ask yourself "Why COAL?" Club begins with "C," the code for 5 is "L" and the fill-in letters are the vowels "O and A."

• **The 6 of Clubs is CASH.**

Again, ask yourself "Why CASH?" Club begins with "C," the code for 6 is represented by "SH" (but it also could have been j, ch, dg, or soft g) and the fill-in letter is the vowel "A."

**• The 7 of Clubs is CAKE.**

Again, ask yourself "Why CAKE?" Club begins with "C," the code for 7 is "K" (but it also could have been Q or hard C) and the fill-in letters are the vowels "A and E."

**• The 8 of Clubs is CUFF.**

Again, ask yourself "Why CUFF?" Club begins with "C," the code for 8 is "F" (but it also could have been V) and the fill-in letters "U and F" (which is a double silent letter).

**• The 9 of Clubs is CUP.**

"C" is used for the suit, "P" for the 9 (but it could have been a "B") and the fill-in vowel "U."

**• The 10 of Clubs is CASE.**

Remember the rule here, a 10 is counted as 0. Therefore you pick up the "C" for the suit and an "S" for the zero (but it also could have been "Z" or soft "C") and the fill-in vowels are "A" and "E."

**• The Jack of Clubs is CADET.**

Again, remember the rule—a Jack is counted as 11, represented by two ones, coded as "D" and "T" (but they could have been 2 "D"s or 2 "T"s). The fill-in letters are the vowels "A" and "E."

**• The Queen of Clubs is COTTON.**

Again, remember the rule—a Queen is counted as 12, represented by a "T or D" followed by an "N." The fill-in letters are the vowel "O" and the silent double letter "T."

**• The King of Clubs is simply CLUB.**

Again, remember the rule—the King is simply the namesake of the suit.

If you clearly understand the reason for each picture-word in the previous 13 cards, you can move on to the suit of Diamonds. Yet, if you don't feel confident about your ability to follow the associations that are leading to each picture-word, then please go through the Clubs again before continuing on.

As you go through the Diamonds, be sure to take the time to understand the reason for each letter that creates the picture-word. The way to do this is to apply the rules of the Phonetic Code with the 6 ground rules for making the picture-words. If you get stuck on the "why" for any of these, simply look at the same numerical card in the Clubs to understand the process. While every picture-word will of course be different, it is created by the same process that you apply over and over again—52 times in fact!

The Ace of Diamonds is DATE.

The 2 of Diamonds is DUNE.

The 3 of Diamonds is DAM.

The 4 of Diamonds is DOOR.

The 5 of Diamonds is DOLL.

The 6 of Diamonds is DISH.

The 7 of Diamonds is DOG.

The 8 of Diamonds is DOVE.

The 9 of Diamonds is DAB.

The 10 of Diamonds is DOSE.

The Jack of Diamonds is DEADWOOD.

The Queen of Diamonds is DETAIN.

The King of Diamonds is simply DIAMOND.

Now let's move on to the suit of Hearts.

The Ace of Hearts is HAT.

The 2 of Hearts is HEN.

The 3 of Hearts is HEM.

The 4 of Hearts is HARE.

The 5 of Hearts is HAIL.

The 6 of Hearts is HASH.

The 7 of Hearts is HOG.

The 8 of Hearts is HOOF.

The 9 of Hearts is HOOP.

The 10 of Hearts is HOSE.

The Jack of Hearts is HEADED.

The Queen of Hearts is HEATHEN.

The King of Hearts is simply HEART.

Now let's finish with the suit of Spades.

The Ace of Spades is SUIT.

The 2 of Spades is SUN.

The 3 of Spades is SUM.

The 4 of Spades is SEWER.

The 5 of Spades is SAIL.

The 6 of Spades is SASH.

The 7 of Spades is SOCK.

The 8 of Spades is SAFE.

The 9 of Spades is SOAP.

The 10 of Spades is SAUCE.

The Jack of Spades is SEEDED.

The Queen of Spades is SATIN.

The King of Spades is simply SPADE.

## Practice with a Deck of Cards

Let's go through these again. But this time, get a deck of playing cards and put them in the same order as shown in the chart. As you turn over each one, verbalize out loud its number, suit and picture-word. Mentally click with the association that connects the number and suit with the picture-word.

*And this time, create your own mental picture in your mind that each card represents.* While most of these are concrete words that can be easily visualized, a few require the techniques of word substitution or sound-alike words to create a concrete image that you can see in your mind.

Take your time. At this point, speed is not important. The goal is to be able to automatically think of the picture-word image when you see the playing card.

The way to do this is to connect with its Phonetic Code by applying the ground rules for making each picture-word.

While right now you are mentally translating each picture-word (much as you would speak a foreign language by translating the word from English), very soon you will "think" in this picture-word language the way you "think" in a foreign language. The more you practice jumping through these associations, the easier and faster you will be able to use this memory system to recall an entire deck of cards.

Let's begin with the suit of Clubs. Say the phrase out loud as you turn over the card and focus on getting that image of the picture-word engrained into your memory. Use your right brain to paint the details of that image with clarity. Visualize a specific cat—tabby, Siamese, black. See a specific shape and color of comb, the car of your dreams, your own birthday cake and more. Take ownership of this system by turning these words into your own personal props.

Beginning with the suit of Clubs, verbalize each line as you turn over the card.

The Ace of Clubs is CAT.
The 2 of Clubs is CAN.
The 3 of Clubs is COMB.
The 4 of Clubs is CAR.
The 5 of Clubs is COAL.
The 6 of Clubs is CASH.
The 7 of Clubs is CAKE.
The 8 of Clubs is CUFF.
The 9 of Clubs is CUP.
The 10 of Clubs is CASE.
The Jack of Clubs is CADET.
The Queen of Clubs is COTTON.
The King of Clubs is simply CLUB.

Now let's move on to the suit of Diamonds.
The Ace of Diamonds is DATE.
The 2 of Diamonds is DUNE.
The 3 of Diamonds is DAM.

The 4 of Diamonds is DOOR.

The 5 of Diamonds is DOLL.

The 6 of Diamonds is DISH.

The 7 of Diamonds is DOG.

The 8 of Diamonds is DOVE.

The 9 of Diamonds is DAB.

The 10 of Diamonds is DOSE.

The Jack of Diamonds is DEADWOOD.

The Queen of Diamonds is DETAIN.

The King of Diamonds is simply DIAMOND.

Now let's move on to the suit of Hearts.

The Ace of Hearts is HAT.

The 2 of Hearts is HEN.

The 3 of Hearts is HEM.

The 4 of Hearts is HARE.

The 5 of Hearts is HAIL.

The 6 of Hearts is HASH.

The 7 of Hearts is HOG.

The 8 of Hearts is HOOF.

The 9 of Hearts is HOOP.

The 10 of Hearts is HOSE.

The Jack of Hearts is HEADED.

The Queen of Hearts is HEATHEN.

The King of Hearts is simply HEART.

Now let's move on to the suit of Spades.

The Ace of Spades is SUIT.

The 2 of Spades is SUN.

The 3 of Spades is SUM.

The 4 of Spades is SEWER.

The 5 of Spades is SAIL.

The 6 of Spades is SASH.

The 7 of Spades is SOCK.

The 8 of Spades is SAFE.

The 9 of Spades is SOAP.

The 10 of Spades is SAUCE.

The Jack of Spades is SEEDED.

The Queen of Spades is SATIN.

The King of Spades is simply SPADE.

Through the Phonetic System you can account for every card in the deck. Like learning a new language, this will take practice to make the picture-words come automatically to you. The following session will help you retain these images in your mind.

## Step 2: Passive Learning Session

The picture-words for the 52 cards are shown on the next page in the order of each of the four suits. Spend the next two minutes gazing at them. As this session is designed for unconscious learning, allowing your mind to wander will give you the maximum benefit. Try not to concentrate on any one item you see.

As your eyes see the picture-word, feel the association pop into your mind that connects the word to the card to the number and letters/consonants of the Phonetic Code. It is not necessary to do these in any order. Just relax and let your mind open as you sweep through the picture-words and recall the deck.

| | | | |
|---|---|---|---|
| CAT | DATE | HAT | SUIT |
| CAN | DUNE | HEN | SUN |
| COMB | DAM | HEM | SUM |
| CAR | DOOR | HARE | SEWER |
| COAL | DOLL | HAIL | SAIL |
| CASH | DISH | HASH | SASH |
| CAKE | DOG | HOG | SOCK |
| CUFF | DOVE | HOOF | SAFE |
| CUP | DAB | HOOP | SOAP |
| CASE | DOSE | HOSE | SAUCE |
| CADET | DEADWOOD | HEADED | SEEDED |
| COTTON | DETAIN | HEATHEN | SATIN |
| CLUB | DIAMOND | HEART | SPADE |

To help lock-in your lesson please play the *Super Memory Transformation* Soundtrack (located on Track #3 of your *Brain Supercharger* CD). Put the book aside for now and make sure to use stereo headphones. Find a comfortable position & quiet place where you can rest undisturbed for the next 30 minutes.

## Step 3: Assessment

You are now ready to test your recall of the 52 cards of the deck. Using your knowledge of the Phonetic Code, you should be able to give the picture-word code for each of the following cards. After you are done, compare your answers to the list of picture-words on the previous pages (each correct answer is worth one point). If you have difficulty remembering any particular card, the ground rules below can give your mind a jump start:

- Each of the picture-words begin with the letter of the suit name.

- The consonant sound following the beginning letter is the Number Code that represents the value of the card.
- Aces have a value of 1, which tells you the picture-word for an Ace has either the letter "T or D" in it.
- The 10 is counted as a 0 rather than combining the two digits of 1 plus 0.
- The picture-word for the King is simply the suit's namesake.
- The Jack is counted as an 11 (represented by two "T"s or 2 "D"s or one of each) and the Queen is counted as a 12 (represented by a "T or D" followed by an "N").

## • 52 Card Recall

CLUBS

Ace _____

2 _____

3 _____

4 _____

5 _____

6 _____

7 _____

8 _____

9 _____

10 _____

Jack _____

Queen _____

King _____

DIAMONDS

Ace _____

2 _____

3 _____

4 _____

5 _____

6 _____

7 _____

8 _____

9 _____

10 _____

Jack _____

Queen _____

King _____


HEARTS

Ace _____

2 _____

3 _____

4 _____

5 _____

6 _____

7 _____

8 _____

9 _____

10 _____

Jack _____

Queen _____

King _____


SPADES

Ace _____

2 _____

3 _____

4 _____

5 _____

6 _____

7 _____

8 _____

9 _____

10 _____

Jack _____

Queen _____

King _____


Your Total Score: _____

If your score was 45 or more you're doing great. If your score was low don't worry. Remember, this process becomes more automatic with practice. If you are not confident of your ability to recall these picture-words, simply repeat Steps 1 and 2 of this workshop.

Knowing the picture-words is the first step in using the Phonetic System to recall the random play of a deck of 52 cards. The second step is to link these cards into a link story, as you did with the first memory system you learned in this course. The next two *Photographic Mind Workshops* will give you practice using the Link System with cards, and show you another memory technique that will improve your ability to play any game of cards.

## Creating a Mental Flip Book of Cards

With the ability to picture the 52 cards in your memory, you are well on your way to improving your odds at any card game. This will allow you to mentally see each card that has been played by linking each card as it is played to the one before it and after it.

To do this, you use the Link System to make a mental flip book of the randomly played cards. You did this in the first *Photographic Mind Workshop* with the eggs sledding on strips of bacon down a hill of frozen milk, etc.

Instead of trying this technique with an entire deck, let's begin first with just 12 cards. These 12 cards (which will be given in a random order in the next workshop) are the 2, 3 and 4 of each suit. These associations are the easiest because there is only one choice of letter in the phonetic code: "N" for 2, "M" for 3, and "R" for 4. Let's review these picture-words here:

The 2 of clubs is a CAN.
The 3 of clubs is a COMB.
The 4 of clubs is a CAR.

The 2 of hearts is a HEN.
The 3 of hearts is a HEM.
The 4 of hearts is a HARE.

The 2 of spades is a SUN.
The 3 of spades is a SUM.
The 4 of spades is a SEWER.

The 2 of diamonds is a DUNE.
The 3 of diamonds is a DAM.
The 4 of diamonds is a DOOR.

To make a flip book from these cards as they are randomly played, you would mentally link each picture-word (representing each card) together in a crazy, illogical, bizarre story that you lock into your memory with emotion. To make this flip book come alive, remember to incorporate the following five guidelines:

1. Inject action into your picture.
2. Use exaggeration by making the items bigger than life.
3. Increase the quantity of the item.
4. Include yourself in the picture (in an illogical way).
5. Be sure to use emotion involving your senses.

## Photographic Mind Workshop: Deal Me In!

## Step 1: Active Learning Session

To enhance your experience of the material please play the *Accelerated Learning Music* soundtrack (located on Track #2 of your *Brain Supercharger* CD) while you complete the following workshop exercise.

During this step you will follow along in your book as you see the 12 cards drawn from the deck. You'll also read the Link story for the picture-words that creates the mental flip book. A little further into the session you'll verbalize the Link story out loud.

You already know that the cards in play will be the 2, 3, and 4 of each suit. You already know their picture-words (refer to the previous page if you need to). All you are waiting for is the order of the cards so that you can link these together in a mental flip book.

Here is that order: the 4 of Hearts, the 4 of Spades, the 3 of Hearts, the 3 of Clubs, the 2 Hearts, the 2 of Clubs, the 2 of Spades, the 2 of Diamonds, the 4 of Clubs, the 3 of Diamonds, the 4 of Diamonds, and the 3 of Spades.

By linking these picture-cards together you could imagine the following flip book.

*The <u>hare</u> ran into the <u>sewer</u>. It was wearing a dress with the <u>hem</u> falling out. A loose string of the hem got caught in a <u>comb</u> being used by a <u>hen</u> who was holding a <u>can</u>. On the can was a picture of a big yellow <u>sun</u>. Inside the can was a sand <u>dune</u>. The dune was spilling out all over the street causing the <u>car</u> you were driving to skid. You rammed the car into a <u>dam</u> and you broke off the <u>door</u>. The <u>sum</u> total to fix the car was very high.*

To remember the cards that were played you simply run through your mental flip book.

## Chunking the Flip Book

The story is going to be repeated again, only this time it will be broken into chunks. Read the chunks, verbalizing each one out loud. As you visualize the mental images of the picture-words as vividly and as clearly as you can.

The <u>hare</u> ran into the sewer.

It was wearing a dress with the <u>hem</u> falling out.

A loose string of the hem got caught in a <u>comb</u>, being used by a <u>hen</u> who was holding a <u>can</u>.

On the can was a picture of a big yellow <u>sun</u>.

Inside the can was a sand <u>dune</u>.

The dune was spilling out all over the street causing the <u>car</u> I was driving to skid.

I rammed the car into a <u>dam</u> and broke off the <u>door</u>.

The <u>sum</u> total to fix the car was very high.

## Step 2: Passive Learning Session

The 12 cards from the Active Learning Session are shown in the order they were dealt. Spend the next two minutes gazing at them. As this session is designed for unconscious learning, allowing your mind to wander will give you the maximum benefit. Try not to concentrate on any one item that you see.

As your eyes see the cards, hear the story play back in your mind as you visualize the mental flip book. Just relax and let your mind open as you sweep through the whole scene and recall the picture-words in the story.

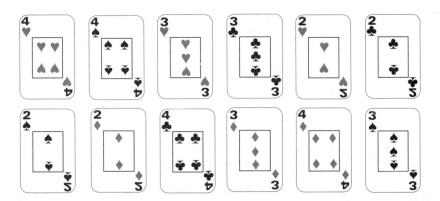

To help lock-in your lesson please play the *Super Memory Transformation* Soundtrack (located on Track #3 of your *Brain Supercharger* CD). Put the book aside for now and make sure to use stereo headphones. Find a comfortable position & quiet place where you can rest undisturbed for the next 30 minutes.

## Step 3: Assessment

You are now ready to test your recall of the order the 12 cards were dealt. Simply replay the flip book in your mind and decode the picture-words to connect you with each of the 12 playing cards. When you are done, compare your list to the answers provided and write your total number of correct answers on the score line (give yourself 1 point for each correct answer).

• **Recalling the Order of the 12 Cards**

1. _____
2. _____
3. _____
4. _____
5. _____
6. _____
7. _____
8. _____

    9. _____

  10. _____

  11. _____

  12. _____

Your Total Score: _____

Did you recall all the cards to get a perfect score of 12? If not, please be patient with your progress. Once you are able to recall this order of the 12 cards, try shuffling them up and coming up with a mental flip book on your own. If you can remember these 12 cards, you can remember all 52 of them. It just takes practice.

## Identifying the Cards that are Still in the Deck

Linking cards to recall their order is a most impressive feat. But it's not all you need to know to win at cards. For in most card games, the secret of winning is in knowing which cards have not been played. And this can be easily accomplished with a technique called mangle.

The mangle idea is faster and easier than linking. All you need to know is your list of picture-words for the cards. When a card has been played, simply call up the picture-word and mangle it in some way or form. *Chop the head off the hen. Cook the hare. Run over the can and crash the car.*

Mangling is easy. And it is effective. To recall the cards that have not been mangled, simply review your deck in *alphabetical order* of suit and in *numerical order within each suit*; meaning go through all the Clubs first, then all the Diamonds, then all the Hearts, and lastly followed by all the Spades. *Whatever image has not been mangled has not yet been played.*

Once you know the mangle technique, it works every time. Which brings up another point: after you've "mangled" one round of cards, you can then "burn" the second round of cards and "drown" the fourth round of cards, and then "paint red" the fifth round of cards. Each round needs to be destroyed in a slightly different manner so you will not get the hands confused!

## Applying the Mangle Technique

Let's try the mangle technique on the 12 cards you used in the previous workshop—the 2, 3, and 4 of all the suits. Read the 12 randomly ordered cards and identify the one that is missing. To make it easier, you will be given the picture-words instead of the cards they represent. As you read each one, mentally mangle it:

> DAM
> SUM
> HEN
> CAR
> DUNE
> SEWER
> CAN
> HARE
> COMB
> HEN
> DOOR

Now, either go through the story to identify the one picture-word that is not mangled, or run through the 2, 3, 4 of each suit to find the missing card. (The missing card is the "sun" or the 2 of Spades.)

At first, using the Phonetic System to remember cards may take some time. But it does work. All it requires is knowing the picture-words backwards and forwards based on their link to the Phonetic Code. <u>This is not memorizing 52 cards. It is reconnecting to the picture-words of the cards based on linking each one through its Phonetic Code.</u> You simply need to organize a new map of these associations in your head by patterning and organizing the deck of 52 cards into categories that will let you quickly access the phonetic code.

# Epilogue

Your course work in the *Photographic Mind* is now complete. Congratulations on the incredible progress you've made by advancing through the four memory systems—the Link, the Loci, the Peg and the Phonetic Systems.

You should be proud of the incredible achievements you've made in boosting your memory power by applying each system to the numerous memory tasks presented in the *Photographic Mind Workshops*. This is especially true of the exercises found in the Advanced Memory Applications which are among the most difficult memory tasks you'll ever encounter.

*Please, keep up your incredible progress.* The statement that was made in the beginning of this book cannot be emphasized enough: People with exceptional memories should be admired for *their motivation* rather than for *their ability*. Memory is a gift we all have. The gift of *exceptional* memory depends on learned rather than innate abilities.

The skills you learned in this program are all you need to know to possess the power of a super memory. With the power of a holographic mind—each memory trace is recorded and retained in the multi-dimensional architecture of your left brain, right brain and your body. This is what a photographic mind is all about. It is a holistic memory of both the intellect of your brain and the emotional memory of your body. Through this balanced support you have a total command of the access routes in your brain and body connecting you to the information and stimuli received through your senses as you come to know your environment.

That information is there for you, stored in free-flowing maps of categories and patterns which serve to organize information in a way that is meaningful to your present needs and desires. Just as memory is essential to our survival, it is also essential that it is stored *not as fixed images,* but as *flexible patterns* that adapt to the new and unexpected, and in so doing <u>create within you</u> a flexibility that will allow <u>you</u> to adapt to the ever-changing environment in which you live.

You are a growing, evolving individual with a phenomenal mind that does so much more than store images or bits of data. A mind that becomes more richly endowed with the capacity to categorize and organize information in connected ways. The real goal and passion of an intelligent mind is not just in knowing more, but reworking, re-categorizing, and putting information together in new and surprising ways. It is important that you remain open to these new and surprising ways as they appear in your life. Because it is through these opportune moments that you will connect with ideas that can lead you to a success that very few people ever come to know.

A far-reaching benefit of a highly trained memory is not in your ability to recall everything you learned, but in the ability to connect with new information, in new and novel ways. How? *Based on the patterning, categorizing, and reorganizing of memories in such a way that you come to know this new information with an uncanny ability and ease.* You are aligned with a force which automatically feeds you knowledge which words simply cannot express.

In essence, it is a knowledge you come to own which you did not know even existed. *It is, perhaps the knowledge of a genius.* A knowing far beyond a super memory, a knowing that only begins to be understood in terms of your holographic mind.

The dramatic increases you have experienced in your memory power during this course are a wonderful achievement, but only a beginning. The ability to improve your memory power is an ongoing advancement. Rather than viewing the end of this course as a destination, see each of the four processes as a way to continue your journey. The way to a powerful memory has been revealed to you. It is now up to you to go forth with all the wonder of a child as you come into the realm of your own potential—not only in the power of your memory, but in the power of your being.

# Appendix
## (What's On Your CD And How To Use It)

This guide explains how to use the unique soundtracks included on your *Brain Supercharger* CD enclosed with this book. Created in a state-of-the-art recording studio, using high-end digital mastering equipment, these soundtracks have been reproduced onto a special glass master and digitally replicated onto the compact disc media. This procedure creates a perfect clone of the original, preserving the special tones and frequencies and insures an extraordinary experience to anyone who uses them. To understand the technology and how to benefit from it be sure to read this entire user's guide before using your soundtracks.

### "Accelerated Learning Music" Soundtrack

Although the philosophy and technology incorporated into your soundtracks share some similar elements, each is used in a different way. The first soundtrack on your CD is titled *Accelerated Learning Music*. It takes advantage of the unique properties of certain musical forms to stimulate learning. It is used in Step 1 (the Active Learning Session) of your *Photographic Mind Workshops* and is designed to help you focus and concentrate on the lesson material.

It is based on the scientific principal that certain musical structures allow students to absorb and retain information quickly and easily—a process first discovered in the 1960s by a Bulgarian scientist named Georgi Lasonov and termed "accelerated learning." The characteristics of this accelerated learning music are found in many pieces of music written in the baroque, classical, and romantic periods.

The tempo of this music falls in a range between 40 and 60 beats per minute, with a simple rhythm pattern of approximately one beat per second. Often called a largo rhythm, this tempo/rhythm combination is similar to the beating of the human heart. The heartbeat of people listening to a largo rhythm will actually slow down to follow the music. This "following response" literally means being in sync with the music.

As your body relaxes to the rhythm of the music, your mind becomes alert in a simple form of relaxation—without telling a muscle to relax, without concentrating on a meditation mantra, without focusing on your breathing. As the music plays, your mind simply opens up.

What's going on here is a kind of "sonic massage" that eliminates the stress of hard mental work. The music helps redirect the focus of your attention inward instead of outward to produce a reverie state. And in this state, students are more relaxed, and amazingly, actually able to learn more in less time.

Another characteristic of *Accelerated Learning Music* is that the melody and harmony of the music are written in a "major" mode. Melody is "a series of pitches that are played one after the other," and harmony is "groups of pitches played simultaneously that enhance the melody." A piece of music written in a "major" mode means that the pitches, represented by musical notes, relate to one another in a way that causes the music to sound a certain way. In a major mode, the music sounds positive or happy, while a minor mode sounds serious, somber, or even sad.

Composers have found that the way you build melody and harmony affects the emotional tone of the music. Each note is a vibration. And the vibration acts on our bodies and minds in either a happy or sad nature.

What we are seeking with this music is to unlock the hidden abilities of the mind by eliminating fear, worry and anger. This in turn, opens you up to a new space (perhaps previously occupied by negative feelings) into which learning can be "poured in" without obstruction.

Through the affective powers of music, a deeper dimension of awareness is achieved. It stimulates positive emotions and drives attention and focus inward. Like a rainbow of vibrational feelings, these emotions (previously neutered by fear and worry) build a bridge into higher awareness.

Although you are instructed in your *Photographic Mind Workshops* to play *Accelerated Learning Music* during Step 1 (the Active Learning Session) you may wish to play it in the background at any time while reading, studying or just relaxing. It is a beautiful piece of music that will stimulate a positive relaxing mood everytime you play it. In addition, mixed into the music are specially recorded affirmations.[1] The voices or whispers you hear are not a defect in the sound recording. They are supposed to be there. Both of the soundtracks on this CD incorporate a "mindscripting" technique whose purpose is to condition your unconscious mind for success. Used regularly they can have a profound impact on your life.

## "Super Memory Transformation" Soundtrack

The second soundtrack on the CD is titled *Super Memory Transformation*, and it uses the *Brain Supercharger* technology.[1] You listen to this soundtrack during Step 2 (the Passive Learning Session) of your *Photographic Mind Workshops*.

Its purpose is to induce a deeply relaxed state of mind. Using a process to facilitate whole brain synchrony and using special mindscripting techniques, it is designed to condition your unconscious with a new set of beliefs about memory, creativity and learning. In addition it will give you an excellent brain massage allowing you to experience profound states of meditation and altered consciousness.

There are a few general points to keep in mind when you use the *Super Memory Transformation* soundtrack. To get the most out of the *Brain Supercharger* technology it is best to use it on a regular basis, daily if possible, for a full 28 minute session. And unless you repeat the experience on a frequent basis, you will not receive the full benefits it has to offer. You will be guided when to use each of your soundtracks as you go through the *Photographic Mind Workshops* in this book. However it is recommended that in addition you should listen to these soundtracks daily if possible to reinforce the memory transformation process.

Once you have experienced the pleasant sensations of deeper relaxation and higher states of consciousness offered by this technology, you will look forward

---

[1] For more information about mindscripting™ and the *Brain Supercharger* technology please refer to the book *Super Brain Power: 28 Minutes to a Supercharged Brain*.

to these short sessions as a welcome "time out."

Try to practice in a place that is quiet and dimly lit. Use a sturdy comfortable arm chair, a firm sofa, or bed that supports your body well and keeps your spine straight. Loosen tight clothing so that you can breathe easily, and allow the blood to flow freely to all parts of your body. Some people like to remove their shoes during practice. If you wear glasses or contact lenses, you may feel more comfortable removing them as well.

## How to Use the Brain Supercharger Technology

Since relaxation is the opposite of tension, the best way to approach the experience is to "just let it happen." The *Brain Supercharger* technology in these recordings will automatically unfold a deep state of relaxation without you doing anything except just relaxing and letting yourself go. Use stereo headphones only when using this soundtrack, and start each session at the beginning of the program. Slowly, as the soundtrack unfolds, the audio matrix is designed to automatically take you from a conscious beta brainwave state down through a relaxed alpha state and into a deep theta state of relaxation and altered consciousness. This will last for about 25 minutes. Then the audio matrix slowly brings you back to the beta conscious state, for a total 28 minute session.

---

### Note:

*Brain Supercharger* soundtracks must be used with a stereo CD player and headphones only. An exclusive sound engineering process used in this recording called a Neuro-Entrainment Matrix,™ induces a deep state of relaxation and altered consciousness. Through the stereophonic process, the sounds are delivered into specific areas of the mind. A good set of stereo headphones is **required** to gain the proper effect from this soundtrack.

---

It is recommended that you listen to your *Brain Supercharger* at least once per day. No specific time or place is required other than to be undisturbed for 30 minutes.

You may wish to keep a written journal of your experiences. After each session, take 15-20 minutes to record your thoughts, feelings, and experiences. Not only is this a valuable process that gives you a formal record of your progression, but the short time you devote to contemplation has many rewards. You will find this time highly creative and useful for problem solving in every area of your life.

## What Kind of Feelings You Can Expect

When accumulated tension flows out of your muscles and other parts of your body, you can anticipate a number of sensations, some of which may be new to you. These can include tingling, a floating sensation, momentary numbness, mild muscle twitches, or feelings of flowing warmth or heaviness. You may find your mind wandering to unexpected thoughts that startle you, or even experience a lucid dream. This is entirely natural since a common result of this altered state of consciousness is increased mental alertness.

Some people may feel themselves dozing off during a session. You are probably not actually sleeping as the audio matrix is holding you in a theta brainwave pattern which is above the threshold of sleep. But because you've lost all "time sense," it may feel as if you've been sleeping. If you are physically or mentally exhausted, you may find it desirable to turn off your CD player and drift off to sleep after your session.

## The Psycho-Physical Benefits of Regular Use

The *Brain Supercharger* technology is based on altered states research and the study of meditation. There is now a tremendous amount of interest by Westerners in the ancient practice of meditation because of the known health benefits. But much more is going on than just relaxing and dealing with your thoughts and emotions. Meditation is a powerful technique for expanding consciousness.

Here is a testimonial regarding meditation by one of the world's most powerful minds:

*"The really valuable thing is intuition.*
*Through meditation I found answers before*
*I asked the question. Imagination is more*
*important than knowledge."* —*Albert Einstein*

For most of us it is difficult to grasp the concept that our so-called normal waking state is neither the highest nor the most effective state of which the human mind is capable. There are other states of vastly greater awareness which one can enter briefly and then return to normal living enriched, enlivened, and enhanced.

To discover such knowledge we have to go very deeply into meditation. And this is very difficult for those who have not internalized the physiological responses required to induce these mental states. Eastern masters have long known of these difficulties. If every aspiring meditator was meditating correctly, the difficult goal of enlightenment would be common instead of rare.

Your *Brain Supercharger* soundtrack offers a solution. By physically driving the listener into a state of deep meditative awareness, it will allow anyone to experience those higher states of consciousness. The relevance of this level of awareness becomes clear when one remembers the aim is not just to become more relaxed and dreamy, but to expand as far as possible the range of states over which one has full conscious control.

Because the now-established benefits of meditation are widely known, many ailments which are the result of stress can be greatly improved within a few weeks of regular practice. Busy, stressed out individuals can center themselves, see situations more clearly, and cope with the daily difficulties of life. The *Brain Supercharger* is a perfect tool for helping to achieve the benefits that deep meditation and higher states of consciousness have to offer.

## How Your Brain Supercharger Soundtrack Works

The brain gives off electrical energy that corresponds to certain states of consciousness. The four kinds of brainwave patterns are really descriptive tags for different wave speeds. Brainwaves are measured in cycles per second. Delta is the slowest of the brainwaves (0-4 cycles per second), usually prominent when you are in your deepest stages of sleep and not dreaming. Theta (4-8 cycles per second), is related to creativity and dream activity. Alpha (8-13 cycles per second) is characterized by a relaxed but alert state. Beta (14-26 cycles per second) is the brainwave state when you are in normal waking consciousness.

Beta, alpha, theta, and delta are the brain's electrical outputs which science can measure and attach some kind of meaning to. Scientists have no idea as to how these "waves" of energy affect the world outside, but they do know how it affects the world inside. Artists, musicians, and athletes are all prolific producers of alpha-theta brainwave patterns. Creativity and strong alpha-theta activity appear to be linked.

Zen monks, yogis, and others who are experienced meditators, have learned to alter their mind-state through training and discipline. They are able to redirect the energies of consciousness and induce the physical brainwave state of theta at will. This deliberate switching-off of external stimuli changes the content of one's awareness. The letting go of one's normal reality expands awareness and controls attention. But the Eastern forms of meditation require years of concentrated practice to advance into these higher forms of awareness. The *Brain Supercharger* through regular use is designed to give you this same ability without spending 20 years training your brain.

How does it achieve this? Just as certain music can affect your mood, it has been discovered that certain soundwaves played in the right frequency combinations will entrain the brain into a specific mind-state. These sound patterns, called a Neuro-Entrainment Matrix, stimulate the brain/mind to match the electrical frequencies in the theta range (4-8 cycles per second), and the result is an altered mind-state.

Layered over this matrix is a mix of environmental sound effects and soothing tones called a Random Sound Harmonic Overlay. Using special effects engineering, certain sounds and tones are directed to the left and right hemispheres of the brain. Because these sounds are processed in different ways by the left and right hemispheres of the brain, this deliberate redirection of sound causes the left brain to slow down, freeing the creative right brain and inducing whole brain synchrony (integration of left and right hemispheres).

And in this state of whole brain consciousness it is believed you can: enhance your creative and intuitive powers, produce significant gains in mental functioning, and expand your potential for learning and growth.

## What You Hear and Don't Hear

The Neuro-Entrainment Matrix is composed of tones in a subsonic frequency range (beneath the threshold of normal human hearing). These tones entrain your brainwaves slowly from a beta consciousness down into the theta range. The low humming sound you may hear in the background of your soundtrack is the Neuro-Entrainment Matrix doing its thing.

The Random Sound Harmonic Overlay (listening medium) was designed using non-repetitive rhythms. It is not music, and therefore may seem boring to a mind that is used to a great deal of stimuli. But because there are no musical patterns to fixate on, the brain slows down. Your mind is then free to focus on the inner you. As a result, you can become more creative and intuitive, increase your mental clarity, boost your personal IQ, and experience general feelings of euphoria.

## What Happens to You in Alpha-Theta

As your *Brain Supercharger* soundtrack mentally relaxes you into a theta consciousness, your body physically relaxes too. Your heart rate decreases and respiration becomes regular and relaxed. Your muscles relax, and your arms and legs become limp. Your attention becomes focused inward while outside distractions seem to melt away. Here are some comments from different people of what the experience feels like to them:

*"An incredible floating sensation."*

*"I feel like I can just let things happen and everything will work out for me."*

*"I feel an increase in energy, and a release in tension."*

*"It's not the same kind of relaxation like lying down and taking a nap. Instead it's a special kind of relaxation. I feel more aware, and it gives me a great feeling of power and concentration."*

*"I feel as though I'd left my body."*

It is believed by many psychologists and neurologists that the brain uses the theta state for psychological and physiological programming. By training the brain to stay in this altered state on a daily basis for a minimum of 30 minutes, you are opening a door to your unlimited self. Listening to this special soundtrack becomes more than just a pleasant experience. The positive change it produces will affect every area of your life.

As you use this program over a period of months, you should notice less overall stress in your daily life. The anxiety-quelling properties of regular meditation are well documented. And your *Brain Supercharger* experience should deliver similar stress reducing results. Plus, if used regularly, these soundtracks can help you perform at optimum levels. After only a few months of use you'll discover subtle but profound shifts in your life. In addition to a significant reduction in stress, you'll feel a heightened awareness and perception of events around you. You'll become more "centered" and experience a greater sense of "aliveness" and "focus" as you engage in your daily activities. This shift is subtle but profound. And the life transforming effects you'll experience over the months and years to come are forever.

## Rescripting Your Unconscious Through Mindscripting™ Technology

Reducing stress, expanding awareness, transforming your inner world are all incredible benefits of regular use of this technology. But there is something even more powerful that you'll be able to experiment with. *Super Memory Transformation* uses a "Mindscripting" technique specific to the goal of improving your memory. Mindscripting is used to help reprogram your beliefs about yourself and how you perceive the world. You should be aware of how this technology is used to rescript negative emotions, unconscious behavior, and condition your mind for success.

The unconscious mind records and stores our experiences. Through repetition, our experiences become learned automatic functions of behavior, like tying your shoes, driving a car, or riding a bicycle. All of these activities begin on a conscious level, but through repetition become scripted into the unconscious mind resulting in habitual behavior patterns.

Our experiences also form our internal images of "self." These inner images of success or failure we have formed about ourselves radiate outward into the world and affect the way we are judged and treated by others. Habits and internal images of "self" are stored on an unconscious level and can be either good for us or barriers to our growth.

Have you ever wondered why change is so difficult? The reason is because years of defeating self-talk, fear, and negative reinforcing experiences have encrusted a mindscript in the unconscious of failure and limitation. Your inner images have become your reality.

For example, if you see yourself as a poor public speaker, your subconscious mindscript will cause you to stutter, stammer, or become nervous during your speech. Likewise, if you see yourself as a great performer and someone who has a natural ability for public speaking, you probably would have no trouble performing in front of an audience. Your unconscious mindscript keeps you acting in a manner that is consistent with your internal images about reality.

## The Secret Behind the Technology

The reason why the Mindscripting Technology™ can be so effective in changing behavior and modifying a person's self-image, is because the behavioral mindscript (positive experiences) are mapped directly onto the unconscious mind. These special mindscripts are recorded onto the soundtrack at a level that is barely audible to the conscious mind, but the unconscious mind hears clearly. Most self-improvement techniques attempt to work only with the conscious mind. The problem with telling only your conscious mind, "I am wealthy" or "I have a good memory" is that it knows you're lying.

One woman who was trying to lose weight with conscious affirmations said, "I have affirmed that I am thin until I am worn out. I knew when I was telling myself those statements that it was obviously not true." Her statements were rejected by the conscious mind and the very opposite of what she outwardly affirmed was manifested. Why? Because the unconscious mind will take your fears and limiting beliefs and in its own way create obstacles and limitations that prevent change from occurring.

The behavioral mindscripts used in the Mindscripting process succeed because they do not produce a mental conflict with your critical conscious mind. The technology bypasses the conscious mind and is picked up by the unconscious only. The unconscious then goes about acting upon this new experience using the scripts as a guide. The most important fact about the unconscious in this regard is this:

*The unconscious mind doesn't know the difference*
*between a real and an imagined experience!*

By bombarding the unconscious with new internal images and experiences, you are literally rewriting your internal mindscript. And then your outward experiences are realigned to match these new inward images of reality. Sounds oversimplified perhaps, but this is exactly how the universe operates.

The unconscious will follow whatever instructions are placed into it. It doesn't pay any attention to whether or not it is acting in our best interests—it just follows the script our experiences and internal dialogue have given it.

---

### KEY POINT

Your thoughts and emotions project an energy into the universe. By learning how to change your internal programming (how you think and see yourself) you can transform your external experiences. The universe automatically aligns to this new positive energy and incredible things begin to happen. The *Brain Supercharger* technology provides a simple, highly effective method for unleashing this power.

---

## Why These Soundtracks are Special

By using the Neuro-Entrainment Matrix, Random Sound Harmonic Overlay, and the Mindscripting Technology, the *Brain Supercharger* soundtrack with behavioral mindscripts, represents a breakthrough in personal development technology.

First, the Neuro-Entrainment Matrix alters your consciousness by coaxing your brain into a theta state. In this special mind-state, you are more receptive to new ideas and experiences. Then, the Random Sound Harmonic Overlay helps nudge your brain into whole brain synchrony. As your left and right brain hemispheres become synchronized, your mind becomes primed and ready for behavioral rescripting. Finally, the Mindscripting Technology, using the special behavioral mindscripts, maps new habits and behaviors directly into your unconscious. As these mindscripts enter your unconscious, they begin to stimulate a dramatic transformation in attitude and behavior. This is why over 500,000 recordings have been made incorporating the *Brain Supercharger* technology. It is by far one of the most powerful self-improvement techniques ever created.

## Questions and Answers

**Q:** What results should I expect from these soundtracks?

**A:** Each person is different, and it will depend on how often you play them as to how quickly you'll see results. Many people will feel an immediate difference in their attitudes and behaviors. However it may require several weeks or even months of daily sessions before you start seeing substantive results. Everyone should have noticed some positive effects within 60 days. Combined with the techniques you've learned in the *Photographic Mind Workshops*, this is a powerful combination that will surely make a positive impact on your memory powers.

**Q:** How often should I use these soundtracks?

**A:** The *Brain Supercharger* should be used once per day for a full 30 minute session. It may seem difficult at first to fit this 30 minutes into your busy schedule. But it will be well worth the time spent if you do. The benefits of stress reduction, heightened well-being, creativity, and mental clarity in addition to any psychological rescripting benefits make this as important as physical exercise is for your body. You should notice significant improvements at work and in your personal relationships. Give it at least 2 or 3 months of regular daily use and see for yourself if these benefits are not worth fitting a 30-minute session into your schedule.

**Q:** What type of CD player and headphones should I use for playing my *Brain Supercharger*(s)?

**A:** The better stereo players and headphones have a better frequency response. You don't need the most expensive equipment in the world to get results with these soundtracks, but a quality system will enhance the experience significantly. The *Brain Supercharger* soundtrack requires stereo headphones. The single most important factor in making this soundtrack effective is the quality of the headphones. The new ultra-light headphones that sit on the surface of the ear may not be as effective as the kind with the strong magnets that completely surround your ear. If you are planning to invest in a quality pair of headphones, get the kind that completely surround your ear. (Prices range from $30-$150.)

**Q:** What is the content of the behavioral mindscripts?

**A:** A listing of the affirmations being used in the soundtracks is listed below:

I learn quickly
I have instant recall of everything I read
All knowledge is available to me
I am wisdom
I am an advanced learner
I am learning faster each day
I like to learn new things
My IQ goes up
I am intelligent and wise
I learn faster each day
I like to read
I am articulate and knowledgeable
I read faster and remember more
I am a student of life
Learning new things comes easily for me
I discover

I am a quick study
I am relaxed and calm
I am wisdom and learning
I remember everything
When I learn new information I focus my attention
I learn faster than others because I'm focused
My memory improves daily
People around me are amazed at my ability to learn
     so quickly
I accelerate my learning
I can do it
I read faster and remember more
I remember everything I see
New concepts come easily for me
I see how things connect
I have an excellent memory
My reading comprehension goes up
I have instant recall
My memory improves
The more I read the quicker I learn
I am an unlimited person
My mind serves me well

**Q:** When is the best time to play my CDs?

**A:** The *Brain Supercharger* requires 30 minutes of undisturbed relaxation. Plan a time when you can give yourself this 30 minutes each day. Take the phone off the hook and lock the door. Many busy people get up a half hour early every morning to plug into their *Brain Supercharger*. It not only gives them the extra 30 minutes, but the resulting mental clarity and focused attention remains with them throughout the day. Others use it after they get home from work and find it helps them relax after a busy day. And some find it works best for them just before going to bed. You can experiment and find the best time for you and your schedule.

**Q:** Why do I hear "voices" on the *Brain Supercharger*?

**A:** Because you are in a focused mind-state, your awareness is actually heightened. You should be able to hear whispers or murmurs, but not be able to consciously make out the specific mindscripts themselves. This is intentional and not a defect in the soundtrack. The frequency and volume threshold of the behavioral mindscripts have been adjusted to insure maximum results.

**Q:** At what volume level should I play my *Brain Supercharger*?

**A:** The best playback volume is at a comfortable level where the sounds themselves are not loud enough to become a distraction to your relaxation.

**Q:** Can I use these CDs while I'm driving?

**A:** DO NOT under any circumstances use either of these soundtracks while driving, or operating any machinery for obvious reasons.

# The Brain Supercharger Technology

Plug yourself into your *Brain Supercharger* soundtrack for 28 minutes each day. As the special audio matrix layered onto the CD unfolds its magic programming—a blissful state of deep relaxation sets in. Almost immediately your mind is launched into an altered states experience. It's as if both mind and body are being launched into another dimension of time and space. And although it feels incredibly good, what's going on under the surface is something quite profound. The secret engineering process behind these amazing soundtracks is based on 3 discoveries as detailed in the book, *Super Brain Power: 28 Minutes to a Supercharged Brain*:

1. The ability to generate certain musical harmonics and sound frequencies with properties that shift mood and activate "right brain" awareness and help whole brain synchrony. It is believed that people who enter this mind state have a greater ability to "rescript" material on a subconscious level.

2. The use of affirmations to direct positive programming to the unconscious to help in rescripting negative self-defeating beliefs. (Your *Brain Supercharger* soundtrack is loaded with powerful mindscripting™ affirmations embedded in the audio matrix.)

3. Holographic 3-D sound design that delivers specific spatial effects into a listener's mind so you "feel" the sounds moving around inside your head.

# Other LifeQuest Book/CD Experiences:

## Super Brain Power
### 28 Minutes to a Supercharged Brain

Learn about the *Brain Supercharger* technology, how it was developed and used by thousands worldwide to zap stress, boost brainpower and unfold profound states of altered consciousness and meditative awareness. Then experience it yourself—firsthand. The companion CD contains two audio soundtracks (*Super Intelligence* & *Mozart Brain Boost*) plus an instruction session by the author on how to create your own private mind lab to benefit from this technology. Includes 19 mind development workshops to awaken right brain awareness and redirect the energies of consciousness. (Book + 1 CD)

ISBN 1-892805-00-6 • *Available Now*

## Ultra-Weight Control
### The Ultimate Permanent Weight Loss System

Everyone knows the secret to permanent weight loss is eating right and ercising on a consistent basis. Then why is it diets don't work? Because they n't address the way the brain is programmed. This breakthrough system d companion CD addresses the core reason why most diets fail and provides et of powerful mind programming tools to re-train the brain for weight loss ccess. (Book + 1 CD)

N 1-892805-22-7 • *Available 4th Quarter 1999*

## The Millionaire's Mind
### Tattoo Success Onto Your Brain Cells

Learn the secret of how to program your success auto-pilot and imprint the essence of a "millionaire's mind" into your subconscious. All self-made millionaires see themselves as winners and project this energy into the world to attract success. The companion CD contains powerful neuro-mapping™ technology to activate "winning feelings" that triggers the right emotions and attitudes to stimulate success actions. (Book + 1 CD)

ISBN 1-892805-21-9 • *Available 4th Quarter 1999*

## Soul Launcher
### Experiencing Out-of-Body Travel

The owner's manual for soul travel. Much more than a guidebook of techniques and process...this step-by-step system teaches you how to redirect the energy patterns of your brain into optimal states for initiating the ultimate voyage. The companion CD uses powerful mind altering technology to help tune the brain into the right frequency window to launch your soul in a true out-of-body experience. You are forever transformed by the self-knowledge that you are more than your physical body. (Book + 1 CD)

ISBN 1-892805-19-7 • *Available 4th Quarter 1999*

## PushButton Meditation

### The Ultra-Meditation System for Transcendence

Learn the secret of how meditation manipulates the energies of consciousness provoking the mind/brain to operate at higher levels of awareness. Use the companion Ultra Meditation CD to experience profound meditative states & ultimately plug your mind into the blissful ecstasy of transcendence and pure consciousness. (Book + 1 CD)

ISBN 1-892805-23-5 • *Available 4th Quarter 1999*

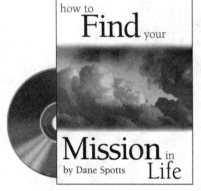

## How To Find Your Mission In Life

Discover your passion and follow your bliss. The special CD workshop not only teaches you how to discover who you are, your passions and ultimately what you should be doing with your life, but takes you through a very insightful "dream discovery" session where using a powerful 3-step process of meditation and guided imagery, you meet your future self and discover your life's purpose. Very powerful and revealing. (Book + 1 CD)

ISBN 1-892805-06-3 • *Available 4th Quarter 1999*

## The Secret of Living a Perfect Life

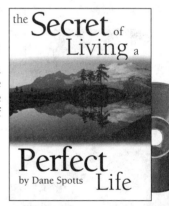

5 key principles guide you to a revelation that will instantly transform your life. Once embraced, these principles expand your possibilities and give you everything you need to live a perfect life. The "secret" that will be revealed to you is a simple but profound truth that will shape every aspect of your life from that moment forward. (Book + 1 CD)

ISBN 1-892805-05-7 • *Available 4th Quarter 1999*

## Mind Power Secrets

Teaches you how to access the hidden powers of your mind to create the future you desire. Using a remarkable mind control technology called "visioneering" it focuses the creative powers of your unconscious to make your dreams come true. Millionaires and peak performing athletes use it to achieve success and you can too. (Book + 1 CD)

ISBN 1-892805-07-3 • *Available 4th Quarter 1999*

# The Brain Supercharger–Mind Lab

## 12 BRAIN SUPERCHARGER "MINDSCRIPTING" SOUNDTRACKS

Get the complete *Brain Supercharger* Mind Lab which includes 12 different titles (each about 28 minutes in length—recorded onto 6 CDs) incorporating the "Supercharger" technology. Different flavors if you will...each designed to train and relax your conscious mind...while opening a doorway into your inner mind.

### 12 Mindscripting Titles To Experiment With

As reported in the book *Super Brain Power*, this mind technology has been used to help reprogram negative beliefs and self-sabotaging behaviors. How? Researchers believe the "alpha-theta" mind-state opens a window into the unconscious. Similar to hypnosis, once a channel is opened, it's possible to transfer positive programming. You'll learn to use the mindscripting technique for rewiring your belief systems and how you see yourself and the world. This is very empowering. Because your mood, emotions, and self-concept result from the way you think. By rescripting your internal dialogue you can shape your perceptions and transform your personal reality. How will you know if it's working? The only way to know for sure is by measuring your personal feelings. The purpose of your Mind Lab (the 12 *Supercharger* titles listed below) is to give you the raw tools to experiment with on yourself. Follow the instructions and keep track of your progress in a journal and prove the results to yourself.

Note: Each *Brain Supercharger* is loaded with powerful mindscripting™ affirmations embedded into the audio matrix. These unique soundtracks have sold for as much as $50 each, which gives the Mind Lab a potential value of $600. As a reader of this book you can receive all 12 titles for half of their original cost...

1. Ultra Success Conditioning
2. Perfect Body Image
3. Project a Winning Self-Image
4. Mastering Stress
5. Unleashing Creativity
6. Healthy Mind/Healthy Body
7. Super Memory & Learning
8. Sports Performance
9. Soaring Self-Confidence
10. Improve Love Relationships
11. Attract Wealth & Prosperity
12. Enhanced Psychic Functioning

Brain Supercharger—Mind Lab™...................................................................$299.95 [US]

| | |
|---|---|
| **TO ORDER** | 800-657-8646 |
| **CUSTOMER SUPPORT** | 425-643-9939 |

**or visit our web page at www.mind-tek.com**

# Ultra Meditation Transcendence System

The Ultra-Meditation 5-Level System for Transcendence was developed to open the mind's gateway to greater levels of awareness by driving your consciousness inward and feeding the brain with a steady flow of psychic energy. As described in the book *Super Brain Power* it is, "The ability to facilitate whole-brain synchrony entirely through sound...by applying the use of certain musical harmonics and sound frequencies, mood can be shifted, 'right brain' awareness activated, and whole brain synchrony promoted." 5 CDs are included in the special boxed set, each with a different audio matrix designed to promote transcendence and peak experiences.

### Ultra Meditation I—The Beginning
Powerful beginning tool for exploring the possibilities of the "theta state."

### Ultra Meditation II—Transformation
Complex audio matrix designed to drive you into a deeper more powerful meditation experience.

### Ultra Meditation III—Awareness
Very subtle but powerful sacred sounds that connect you to an aboriginal dream-time meditation.

### Ultra Meditation IV—Cetacean Mind Link
Connect your consciousness to the audio world of whales and dolphins.

### Ultra Meditation V—Near Death Experience
Take your consciousness beyond & back to explore the 5-step process of a near death experience.

The Ultra Meditation 5-Level system for transcendence is the ultimate mind expanding audio experience.

**Ultra Meditation 5-Level Transcendence System™**......................................$199.95 [US]

| TO ORDER | 800-657-8646 |
|---|---|
| CUSTOMER SUPPORT | 425-643-9939 |

**or visit our web page at www.mind-tek.com**

# The MindQuest Meditation Computer

**Relax and Explore Alternate Mind States With Push-button Control**

## Technical Specifications

- **Fully Programmable Frequency Matrix** (1-30cps)
- **4 Built-In Sound Effects** (rain, stream, crickets, surf)
- **20 Memory Positions** (For Storing Your Custom Meditation/Mind Programs)
- **10 Preset Programs** (Automatic programs)
- **Adjustable Program Times**
- **Adjustable Pitch Range**
- **External Audio Input**
- **Thousands of Program Combinations**

## MIND MACHINE BREAKTHROUGH

After a hard day at the office, you owe yourself a good mind massage, so you plug in the Thunderstorm soundtrack into your MindQuest™ meditation computer. Punch in the code for a heavy duty relaxation session, and instantly launch your consciousness into another time and place. After only a few moments, you're sucked into an amazing virtual dream-state. Images, colors, and patterns are created on the insides of your closed eyelids while off in the distance you hear the rumblings of a great thunderstorm. The mental imagery is so strong it feels as if your mind and body are one...being pulled into the eye of the storm.

### Amazing Light/Sound Effects

The powerful light/sound matrix stimulates your imagination like nothing you've ever experienced. And because it's computer controlled, you can experiment with thousands of different frequency combinations. Plus there are four incredible mind-blowing sound effects (rain, mountain stream, crickets, and surf) actually built into the on-board computer chip along with adjustable time parameters and pitch range. The programmable frequencies give you amazing pushbutton control over your meditation. The size of a pocket calculator the MindQuest is completely portable so you can use it to meditate and relax while traveling too.

### Incredible Mind Journeys

Using proven light/sound sensory technology, the MindQuest allows you to experiment with different audio and light stimulation effects designed to unfold profound relaxation and unleash the powers of your imagination. A spectacular light show is orchestrated within the sound matrix and projected into your mind's eye. The result? Your consciousness is automatically launched into an incredible inner universe. Experience the ultimate meditation and dream machine, and take your mind on the ultimate mind journey.

### Bonus Soundtracks Included—FREE

*Each kit includes computer, headphones, light-pulse glasses, AC adapter, and four virtual dreamscape soundtracks.*

**MindQuest™**........................................................................**$199.95 [US]**

**TO ORDER** `800-657-8646`

**CUSTOMER SUPPORT** `425-643-9939`

WARNING: For Experimental Purposes. The MindQuest Uses Powerful Light/Sound Technology That Can Potentially Induce Seizures in Susceptible Individuals, Including Those With No Prior Seizure History.

**or visit our web page at www.mind-tek.com**

# Want To Join The Club?

WE ARE VERY INTERESTED in what you think of the ideas and technology presented in this book. And we'd like to hear your opinions and comments. On the following page is a brief questionnaire, which you can fill out and return to us (or if you like you can visit us on online at www.mind-tek.com). Your comments will be kept confidential unless you give us permission to use them.

If you do us this favor of providing your feedback, we'll automatically enroll you in our *Mind Warrior's* club. A group of like-minded individuals who connect online to share their experiences and are working toward the evolution of their consciousness and the consciousness of our planet. As a member/subscriber you'll be able to participate in our online/web conferences and link up with others on a similar path.

In addition to the web conferences, there are plans to offer online workshops and teaching forums on emerging mind development technologies and related subjects of interest. It's something you'll want to be a part of as we cross over into the new millennium.

**visit our web page at www.mind-tek.com/forum**

# Registration Card

Name: _____

Address: _____

City/State/Zip: _____

What is your email address: _____

Book Title: _____ **The Photographic Mind** _____

How did you learn about this book? _____

❑ recommended by a friend        ❑ received ad in mail
❑ read book review               ❑ saw in catalog
❑ saw in bookstore               ❑ recommended by store clerk

Where did you purchase this book? _____

Please check the top two factors that influenced your decision to buy this book.

❑ cover          ❑ price          ❑ ideas presented
❑ author         ❑ the bonus CD   ❑ other

Would you like to be placed on our preferred mailing list? ❑ yes ❑ no

❑ **Yes, I would like to see my name in print.** You may use my name and quote me in future products and promotions. My phone number is: _____

Comments: _____
_____
_____
_____
_____

Fold Here

- - - - - - - - - - - - - - - - - - - - - - - - - - - - - - - - - - - - - - - - - - - - - - - - - -

Place
Stamp
Here

**Attn: Book Projects Group**
**LIFEQUEST BOOKS**
**P.O. Box 1444**
**Issaquah, Washington 98027**